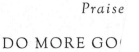

Praise

DO MORE GO

"Thoroughly inspiring and motivating. Challenging the convention that to be a leader you need to have followers, the book very effectively inspires true leaders to uncover the greatness in *every* individual. In this engaging book, Steve Scheier goes to the heart of leadership to reveal that qualities such as integrity, empathy, humility, and passion are essential for anyone who wants to harness the talents of others to accomplish a shared goal. Those seeking an inclusive leadership model will discover much value in these pages."

—ROBYN C. SCATES, CEO, LAW Academy for Women

"This is the book that the nonprofit sector's leadership needs, whether they know it or not. Scheier identifies one of the nonprofit sector's key vulnerabilities—the lack of clarity on who has the power and who makes the decisions—which leads to inefficiencies, confusion, and conflict. He offers a roadmap for creating a new leadership dynamic that confronts fears and biases, provides a shared language and methodology, and taps into the power that a passion for cause produces. *Do More Good. Better.* nails what nonprofit leaders need to move their organizations into the new realities of the 21st century."

—CYNTHIA MURRAY, President and CEO, North Bay Leadership Council

"Steve goes straight to the heart of the core issues of every social sector organization. This happens everywhere, yet no one has hit the nail on the head with this clarity. When we experience these common issues, we blame the leader or churn the staff, which is such a waste of energy and resources. Finally, a direct, solutions-oriented book for our social sector that will help us all stay in the game and feel rewarded as we do great work."

—JULIE CASTRO ABRAMS, Founder and CEO, Bay Area Women Leader's Network;
Member of the Board of the Women's Funding Network

"'Employee empowerment' without the ability to make or contribute to important decisions is a hollow exercise. Steve Scheier strips the veneer off the current limitations of nonprofit decision-making and provides a tool to make employee empowerment a reality."

—CHIP CONLEY, Joie de Vivre founder;
New York Times bestselling author of *Emotional Equations*;
Head of Global Hospitality and Strategy at Airbnb; nonprofit board member

"This book removed the scales from my eyes and taught me that nonprofits are a different beast—in distribution of power, relationships with constituencies, and employee recruitment and retention. If you want to optimize the leadership of a nonprofit, this is the hands-on guide to help you succeed."

—GUY KAWASAKI, Chief Evangelist of Canva
and former Chief Evangelist of Apple; board of trustees, Wikimedia Foundation

"Steve crafts a compelling and powerful roadmap for nonprofit leaders, staff, and board members who want to learn how unexamined power and decision-making processes in their organization may be hampering their mission-focused efforts. Incorporating his framework with real-life examples and providing readers with space for reflection, Steve drives home the notion that everyone in a nonprofit has the capacity to learn, change, and lead by first understanding the role of power relations and decision-making. Written in an engaging and clear style, this captivating and thought-provoking book is a must-read for all nonprofit practitioners as well as for nonprofit management students."

—JUDITH Y. WEISINGER, PH.D.,
Associate Professor, Business & Nonprofit Management Researcher, Mills College

"Engaging and uniting an organization—while minding the world outside that you're trying hard to serve—is no easy or intuitive feat. Steve lays down a language and framework to find ease where you can and gain the results you need to grow as an organization, all lovingly and so well delivered here in his book."

—B.J. MILLER, M.D., Executive Director, Zen Hospice Project

"This book nails the inherent tension in the social sector around power—who has it, who doesn't, and what we do with it—and offers an incredibly important conversation the nonprofit sector is often deeply uncomfortable with. *Do More Good. Better.* brings an intentionality and normalcy to a discussion that is often fraught with challenge for social change leaders, and its actionable concepts could be game-changing for social entrepreneurs, people of color, and anyone who loves and supports a mission."

—KARLA MONTERROSO, Vice President of Programs, CODE2040

"It is abundantly clear that Steve understands the nuances of nonprofit leadership. He has created an effective roadmap for leaders—a guide that clearly identifies the path to confident advocacy, decisive decision-making, and sustainable success through collective engagement. This courageous book is a beacon of light for leaders who desire to change the current culture in their organizations with confidence and clarity."

—JAMILA A. MINDINGALL, Founder & CEO, Bedrock Resourcing Group

DO MORE GOOD.
BETTER.

DO MORE GOOD. BETTER.

Using the Power of Decision Clarity® to Mobilize the Talent of Your Nonprofit Team

———————◆———————

STEVE SCHEIER

Illustrations by G.E. Gallas

High Impact Press

ISBN: 978-0-9962894-0-5

Published by
High Impact Press
San Francisco, CA

Edited by Taylor Ray and Stacey Aaronson
Book design by Stacey Aaronson
Illustrations by G.E. Gallas

Printed in the USA

In loving memory of Amy Doppelt.
Her courage and love made everything possible.

And for Heather, Lauren, and Sprout.

TABLE OF CONTENTS

Foreword | i

Introduction | 1

PART ONE: **EXPLORING THE FRAMEWORK, FEARS, AND CHALLENGES INHERENT IN THE NONPROFIT ENVIRONMENT**

CHAPTER 1: Three Surprises About Power and Decision-Making | 9

CHAPTER 2: Understanding the Roles of Power and Decision-Making | 23

CHAPTER 3: Your Decision-Making Ecosystem | 59

CHAPTER 4: Dealing with Conflict | 85

PART TWO: **REFOCUSING AND RE-ENERGIZING YOUR ORGANIZATION USING DECISION CLARITY**

CHAPTER 5: How Decision Clarity Can Transform Your Organization | 109

CHAPTER 6: Finding Decision Clarity Allies | 121

CHAPTER 7: Step One – Inventorying Decisions | 139

CHAPTER 8: Step Two – Prioritizing Decisions | 153

CHAPTER 9: Step Three – Self-Advocacy | 173

CHAPTER 10: Creating Decision Clarity Grids | 191

CHAPTER 11: Step Four – Engaging and Communicating | 213

CHAPTER 12: The Decision Clarity Architect | 231

Conclusion | 245

Index | 247

Acknowledgments | 251

About the Author | 255

About Scheier+Group | 257

FOREWORD

The day I met Steve Scheier was a lucky day, but it was not a day I was looking forward to. I had called upon Steve, who was the vice president of human resources, to help facilitate a difficult conversation between my executive director and me. Although I had requested the supervised meeting, I only did so because it was the recommended protocol in the large nonprofit where I worked. I had little hope that the involvement of HR was anything but a formality, and I was certain that in the end, my voice and my perspective would go unheard.

I sat at the table feeling alone and outnumbered by race and gender, as two white men with more organizational power than I had waited for me to speak. I thought to myself, *Choose your words carefully, because Mr. Scheier will protect the status quo. He's "the man" in this corporate nonprofit, and I'm just an on-the-ground deliverer of services.*

But the man who would later write this book—about how power and decision-making can be wielded responsibly—surprised me. To my amazement, Mr. Scheier was the most objective, clear, transparent, and fair tie-wearer I'd ever met. He shot my assumptions right out of the water, and he addressed the issue with a clear understanding of equity, shared decision-making, and next steps.

That day was fortuitous because years later, Steve and I had the chance to work together on bringing Decision Clarity® to life. Over the course of three years, I've had the opportunity to further understand the intricacies of this method—an innovative, systematic, and practical model designed to support nonprofit leaders as they make real social impact, and heed the call to change the world.

What draws me to this work is its ability to confront the stifling power dynamics surrounding race, gender, class, sexuality, access, and privilege. Steve's four-part IPAC 4 Impact model allows these elements often left in the dark to come into the light. It confronts the code of silence about who has power and how decisions are made, and it offers a process for clearly and professionally advocating for greater decision-making influence.

In addition, Decision Clarity takes special care to speak specifically to an executive director's understanding of power in her or his organization, as well as to explore how race, gender, and privilege affect power and decision-making in nonprofits. Steve also speaks about the difficult-to-discuss topic of implicit bias and how it impacts all our decision-making.

This book and the Decision Clarity process are extraordinary in that they speak to *all* nonprofit stakeholders—what Steve appropriately calls our "decision-making ecosystem." While the book is primarily directed at officially titled nonprofit leaders such as executive directors, board members, and other managers, it's vital to understand how the rest of us can influence our organizations in unprecedented ways.

Put simply, the status quo will remain the status quo unless those who see the value and necessity of disruption confront their fears and have the courage to, well, disrupt. This book provides a guide on how to do that; it also offers a standard to use to determine whether or not we want to extend our talents to a particular organization, even if its mission is one we hold dear.

In your hands, you hold a recipe for a nonprofit movement, one that will allow you to do the work you're doing to make this world better, without the usual burnout, fatigue, murkiness, and inequity. Decision Clarity is a blueprint, a do-gooder's map to clarifying power and decision-making in nonprofits, so that the work we have chosen to do—to create opportunities and improve lives—doesn't kill us in the process. A must-have guide to enhance and grow our abilities to effectively change the world, this book will deftly enable you to do more good, better.

Diedra Barber, MBA, Chief Business Development Officer, Scheier+Group
Founder of Filament Consulting Group, Oakland, CA

INTRODUCTION

I want to start an unexpected and important movement in the nonprofit sector, one that will revitalize every person in measurable, influential ways, enabling them to love their jobs more and to do more good in the world. This may sound bold, but it's completely achievable, and I'm going to show you how.

Whether you're an executive director, board member, leader, staff member, or volunteer, you work in or give your time to a nonprofit because you want to make the world a better place. But most who work in nonprofits often feel they're spinning their wheels, merely keeping their heads above water, and frustrated because they don't have a blueprint for working more efficiently with their teams. It's a genuine challenge, and it all stems from two crucial facets that affect everything within an organization: power and decision-making.

From my years of experience working with nonprofits, I know without a doubt that if nonprofits rethink and improve these two practices, they will use their existing human and financial resources more effectively, which is a goal of everyone in the philanthropic arena. That may sound like a simple formula, but the truth is that there has never been a framework to help nonprofits achieve this ... until now.

Despite the presence of strategic plans and organization charts, many nonprofits are operating less than efficiently because they maintain outdated decision-making practices. Let me be clear here that those in power have difficult jobs; I've merely observed that most leaders don't know how to engage in conversations about *who* has decision-making power and who *should* have decision-making power, openly and without fear. And it's not about making "better" decisions, though that's important, it's about determining who gets to make the decisions that need to be made, and the process they use to get there.

Nonprofits have important missions and difficult goals, and this book can help you achieve them by eliminating decision-making confusion and reducing conflict. Where do power and decision-making confusion and conflict exist in nonprofits? Everywhere.

Beginning at the top, many executive directors face boards that underperform and are confused about what power they have and what responsibilities they should take on. Nonprofit boards run the gamut from checked-out to micromanaging. The result? Very few are thought to operate efficiently.

Nonprofit leaders often rely on concentrated decision-making models, where they alone determine the questions facing the organization, and then fail to use the decision-making capabilities of their entire staff. Other leaders rely on a consensus-based approach to maintain an idea of harmony, simultaneously hobbling the organization's ability to act. All the while, employee attrition is high, board seats are unfilled, and executive directors are grinding themselves into exhaustion.

And while the status quo may not be efficient or effective, people are afraid to challenge how decisions are made in their organizations. This resistance to deal with power and decision-making directly is understandable. People in nonprofits operate on a shared vision; no one wants to be alienated from the group. But this fear of rejection can have a paralyzing effect on the ability to improve decision-making—especially when there is no shared language for how to talk about it, and no established guidelines for how to do it.

Even when power and decision-making responsibilities are somewhat clear in an organization, decision-making unrest is common. In the absence of a clear, consistent, and non-threatening way to *advocate* for it, people inefficiently and surreptitiously wrestle for power and authority. These internal debates create dysfunction, conflict, stymied leaders, and frustrated and disempowered staff.

In our society, we talk a lot about "employee empowerment"—a well-intentioned concept. But in most organizations, empowerment is a catchphrase that means precious little. Many people find their workplaces to be stifling and their work experience to be frustrating. And while the goal of being actively involved in your organization may be desirable, the methods for *accomplishing* it are often not well understood or easily implemented.

The irony is that unless you can get clear about your power and decision-making responsibilities, *and* you have a straightforward process for advocating for the decisions you want to make (or support), empowerment is a vague concept that leads to a feeling of being *dis*empowered. Organizations that contain disempowered people can't operate at the levels necessary to build sustained success. This book offers a practical way out of this trap.

Organizations that clarify power and decision-making reap other benefits as well. Our experience indicates that those who pursue this approach make faster and more considered decisions. And because more people are involved in the substantive nature of decision-making, organizations do a better job of attracting and retaining talent. When people are offered real opportunities to make decisions, they understandably become even more committed to their mission; they're likewise less frustrated, because they have more ability to make a difference. What's more, being able to tell recruits that your nonprofit is committed to clarified decision-making gives you a competitive advantage. The result is that good people are prone to come to your organization and stay. Churn is reduced, saving both time and money.

Another vital advantage of clarifying power and decision-making was detailed in a recent issue of *Nonprofit Quarterly*. Stating what everyone knows but few have been willing to say, the article details how "at least 60% of the people nonprofits serve are people of color ... [but] whites lead 9.5 out of 10 philanthropic organizations."[1] These numbers don't reflect a conscious conspiracy to silence people of color or deny them leadership opportunities, but these facts did not come into being, and do not persist, by accident. In most cases the leadership realities of nonprofits simply reflect the inherent advantages that whites already have in our society—they have more economic power so they can afford to take the lower salaries that nonprofit service entails; they also go to college at higher rates than people of color so they are better positioned to ask for support from people who also went to college and have money.

While this makes "sense" on one level, these "realities" perpetuate our existing power and decision-making structures. So while there is a good deal of diversity at the lower levels of these same organizations, we're simply not providing enough leadership opportunities for them. The bottom line: although we need more diverse leaders, staff members of color are not being raised up to higher positions in numbers that will make a difference.

---

[1] Dubose, Derwin. "The Nonprofit Sector Has a Ferguson Problem." *NonProfit Quarterly*, December, 2014.

Women also suffer from the same lack of leadership opportunities, as well as the chance to weigh in and make the big decisions facing the sector. A 2012 study out of the University of Denver found that "among nonprofits with budgets in excess of $25 million, women constitute only 21% of the leadership roles, even though they make up 75% of the (nonprofit) workforce."[2] Guidestar provides further historical insight into the status of women leaders in nonprofits through their 2014 report, saying that while "the majority of organizations with budgets of $1 million or less have women as CEOs, female representation in that (CEO) role declines as budget size increases. Only 17% of organizations with budgets of more than $50 million had female CEOs in 2012."[3] This shows that women are clustered in small nonprofits, many of which they founded, but have disproportionately smaller representation in large organizations. Why is that?

As mentioned above, there are a number of economically oriented reasons for this phenomenon, but another is that many people have unconscious bias about who has and should have power—and who makes and should make decisions in our organizations. These unconscious biases hamper women and people of color, and as a result, they often have to move on to roles in other organizations in order to achieve higher positions and greater decision-making authority. This movement not only hurts the organization they are leaving, but it prevents these individuals from developing a long track record in a single institution, making them seem nomadic. In other words, by leaving their organizations for opportunities they can't pursue in their current jobs, the frequent shifting gives the impression that these committed people are actually *less* committed, further stymieing their advancement and undercutting their ability to persist in their area of specialty. By creating opportunities for decision-making for *all* members of your team, you're providing an inherent advantage to your organization.

In our work at Scheier+Group, we partner with nonprofit and social-impact organizations to clarify power and decision-making. We call our method Decision Clarity, and it is our process for helping nonprofits achieve greater traction. There are other decision-making models that nonprofits can use, but these models don't disturb the status quo; instead, they tend to reinforce it. Our goal is to utilize the decision-making capabilities

---

[2] "The Current State of Women in Leadership." Women's College of the University of Denver, 2012 Report.

[3] "Gender Gap Still Prevalent in Nonprofit Sector." Guidestar report, 2014.

of *everyone* in the organization, and to create a way for people to engage around this difficult topic—not to reinforce structures that already don't work, or at the very least are inefficient. With its focus on driving decision-making down in organizations, Decision Clarity naturally creates more diverse nonprofit leaders, benefiting the sector and the people you serve.

This book is primarily directed to nonprofit leaders and board members, because the majority of changes to power and decision-making must be led and supported by the people who currently have power. However, if you don't have a formal leadership role, this book is also for you. Regardless of your current position within the organization, you can encourage your team to implement a clarified decision-making environment by bringing the ideas in this book to your colleagues and leadership, and advocating for their adoption.

Our company goal is to help mission-driven organizations empower their people in significant, practical ways so they can do more with less, and ultimately do more good. We could spread our message one consulting engagement and Boot Camp at a time, but the nonprofit sector can't wait. We believe that the work of nonprofits is vital to humankind; they must be given every opportunity to succeed. It's therefore crucial that the ideas we present here penetrate the cultures of nonprofits *now*, for the benefit of everyone involved.

Do More Good. Better. doesn't pull any punches. It advances ideas and principles that some may find uncomfortable, and even provocative. You will be asked to think and act differently, and to challenge assumptions and biases about who has power and who should make decisions in your nonprofit, but the results will far outweigh the effort. The positive transformation of your leaders and staff will be invaluable, and the sleepless nights, persistent overwhelm, and sense you're never doing enough will dissipate as you harness the full potential of your entire team.

By challenging our conventional views of power and decision-making, our society can tackle the issues that matter most. And the good news is that this work can be done *without* hiring more people or spending more money. It simply takes courage to initiate positive change.

Are you in?

PART ONE

Exploring the Framework, Fears, and Challenges
Inherent in the Nonprofit Environment

1

THREE SURPRISES ABOUT POWER
AND DECISION-MAKING

———————◆———————

Have you noticed that sometimes the biggest organizational problems are *so* big that they slowly become invisible? This is precisely why the topics of power and decision-making are so difficult to broach. When we ask people who work in nonprofits about how decisions are made in their organizations, they initially respond in one of five ways:

1. "Decision-making isn't our problem; we just need to figure out how to work better together."

2. "Hmm, I've never thought much about it."

3. "I don't think I can talk about it—it's uncomfortable."

4. "I see how decisions get made, but unfortunately, I don't have the power to change how it works."

5. "We have our problems, but there's nothing we can do about it. Our mission, by nature, involves many different stakeholders. It's complicated, and it will always be complicated."

If you have power, you may not spend much time thinking about how day-to-day decision-making occurs in your organization. If you *don't* have power, you probably think about it more often, but don't know what to do to change it.

Decision-making is always tied to how we think about power and our ability to talk about it. But, our ability to do so is linked to how much influence we have, and the permission we feel to express it both in our organization and in the world.

As B.J. Miller M.D., the executive director of the Zen Hospice Project, said, "I wouldn't have thought decision-making was our key challenge, and yet talking about decision-making has revealed many of our underlying problems."

When I describe the work my team and I do, most people are intrigued to discover how a new and focused approach to decision-making can enhance organizational efficiency; they are likewise often surprised to learn how much leverage they can get by clarifying it so that they can better achieve their strategic plans and serve their overall mission. What's more, most individuals are excited to find that there's a way of thinking and talking about decision-making that will improve staff morale and cohesion. Many people even find new energy, knowing there is indeed a way to approach this topic with their board, leadership team, or staff.

Consider the following questions:

* ❖ Wouldn't your job be more productive if you knew *who* in your organization was making *what* decisions, and you trusted them to do so?

* ❖ Wouldn't your day be easier if you had time to focus on the really important decisions that would advance your organization?

* ❖ Wouldn't life be easier if you knew what decisions you were going to make, and which your board would make?

By utilizing our methodology that works to bring people together to talk about what's most important, the above are just a few of the tensions that get resolved. Best of all, it is straightforward, easy to learn, and action centered.

Whether you are an executive director[4], a manager, a board member, or a staff member, our blueprint will provoke new insights and offer you a chance to clarify your thought process and advocate for new roles. But before we get to that, let's take a look at what makes power and decision-making so challenging to sort out, and sometimes so hard to see.

THE LEADER'S DILEMMA

Leaders of nonprofits have one of the toughest jobs in the world. If you direct a nonprofit, you already know the things that keep you up at night. A short list may look like this:

1. Do we have enough funds in the pipeline?

2. How can we serve more people?

3. How can we improve our program delivery?

4. How can we better quantify our results?

5. How can I keep my team engaged?

6. Is there a way to maximize the involvement of our board without encouraging them to micromanage?

7. How do we hire the right people?

When you lead a nonprofit, it's easy to feel like the weight of the world is on your shoulders. Regardless of how hard you try, you'll never be able to do enough; no matter how much effort you devote to your work, someone will always have another suggestion, demand, or argument that you feel obligated to incorporate, making it tricky to stay on the course you've plotted.

---

[4] We use the term "executive director" to describe the most senior staff leader in a nonprofit. In recent years, nonprofit boards have begun to bestow CEO titles on the people leading their organizations. For our purposes, the two titles are interchangeable.

Leading a nonprofit also means navigating a maze of interlocking decisions, rife with human sensitivities, that can render decision-making both time-consuming and inefficient. For example, take a look at the following statements, made by real people, describing how decisions are made in their nonprofit organizations. Take note as to whether you find these statements familiar or applicable to your own organization.

- ❖ "Everything is a group decision. We like consensus. We don't want to disagree."

- ❖ "When my executive director feels a subject is important enough, she will make the final decision. Actually, she makes about 75% of all our decisions."

- ❖ "We take a long time to mull over decisions, and we constantly revisit decisions we've made."

- ❖ "If someone questions what we've decided, we immediately think we've done something wrong."

- ❖ "As the executive director, I'm always trying both to maintain the hierarchy and arrive at consensus."

- ❖ "Our fear of failure hampers our decision-making and our results."

- ❖ "I feel so isolated in my executive director role."

While it would seem that each quote points at a process issue and the enormous frustration people have with inefficiency, there's no denying that each organization on this list may function better if they had a sounder process for making decisions. But since most leaders struggle with this, let's look a little deeper to examine three surprising aspects of nonprofit decision-making.

THE FIRST SURPRISE

Each of the above statements is different, but they all point to the same underlying element: fear. You hear it in each quote: fear of failure, fear of upsetting organizational harmony, fear of making a mistake, fear of saying no, fear of letting go, fear of stepping on others' toes, fear of challenging authority, fear of appearing weak.

Making a decision is an act of power, and with the exercise of this power comes a slew of emotions that people find hard to manage.

What if I haven't consulted the right people?

What if my decision is the wrong one?

What if others perceive me as not valuing them if I don't include them?

What if others see me as power hungry?

What if they think I'm not qualified to make the decision?

What if I make a huge mistake?

What if they question my motives?

What if I make the wrong decision and innocent people suffer?

What if I make a decision and it goes bad, and then I'm accused of making the wrong decision because of my race, class, gender, or sexual orientation?

THIS IS THE FIRST SURPRISE ABOUT POWER AND DECISION-MAKING:

It is an act of power that often provokes fear.

But fear is like gravity. You can pretend it doesn't exist, but there are unpleasant consequences to ignoring it. Typically, we see three major fears with decision-making: fear of failure, fear of conflict, and fear of rejection.

Fear of Failure

One of the biggest drivers that complicates decision-making and creates subsequent bottlenecks, fear of failure manifests in two ways: societal and personal.

Nonprofits take on huge goals—to end hunger, eliminate homelessness, end illiteracy, to name a few. They take on challenges that no for-profit company would ever attempt. For-profits are "successful" if their sales are increasing and their market share is growing. On the contrary, nonprofit organizations are rarely satisfied with their progress to date. Why? Because there's always another client to serve, another problem to solve—the needs are seemingly never-ending. Success always appears to be around the corner, no matter how much good is being done, and the stakes are always high. What's more, people who lead nonprofits feel that the societal inequities they work to address are so big that failure can't be tolerated. They see the constant challenges faced by their clients, and they don't want to let them down.

On a personal level, people who lead nonprofits also fear disappointing the people and institutions that have given them time and money. There is enormous competition for resources, and no nonprofit can take for granted a steady stream of support. Executive directors and their teams fear that if they fail to deliver results, they won't continue to garner support for their organization —and they will fail not only the clients, but their funders too.

With these societal and personal pressures in evidence, it's not a surprise that executive directors and their teams fear failure. And as a response to that fear, they often concentrate real decision-making power in the hands of a limited number of people. Even when executive directors appear to give decision-making to other parties, they will often pull it back at the first sign of trouble. This practice undercuts the development of other people who could be making these decisions; it also obscures the fact that "protecting" decisions can become a long-term *liability* to the organization.

The fact that so few people in an organization actually have real power can also be embarrassing to those who lead nonprofits, so they may hide this fact under code words such as "collaboration," "shared decision-making," and "consensus building." As one executive director said to me, "I'd rather my people didn't understand that *I* really have all the decision-making authority."

On the staff level, fear of failure is also at play. Even though the pressures on staff may not be as great as what the executive director experiences, people still worry that they may not be making the right decisions, or that their decisions may not have enough support, or that if they fail, they will disappoint their leaders or make a mistake that harms the organization. In organizations with a powerful executive director, staff will get a clear message that vital decisions are too important for them to make and simply stay clear of them.

Fear of Conflict

People generally don't enjoy conflict, but in nonprofits, an aversion to conflict can be a byproduct of the familial atmosphere of the organization.

As J.B. Schramm, Chair of Learn to Earn at New Profit and co-founder of College Summit said, "Looking at my own experience as a leader, there were times when I handled staff with kid gloves, concerned because they were working very hard for less money than they could make in the for-profit sector. Upon reflection, I realized that was a myth—and a little patronizing."

On the staff level, fear of conflict can be a powerful force. Within a familial environment, consensus and harmony are important, and no one wants to feel ostracized from the group for violating the established norms. Staff are slow to question the existing process, and even more reticent to take on decision-making roles unless they are explicitly encouraged to do so.

This topic can get even more complicated by the fact that nonprofit staff fight to gain power for their clients, but often hesitate to talk about the inequities of power within their organizations (and the tortured decision-making that flows from this conflict). Around power, there is often a code of silence that everyone upholds.

These feelings are further complicated by the unresolved and often awkwardly discussed issues of race, gender, class, age, and sexual orientation. This can be compounded in nonprofits, where there may be more diversity than in for-profit organizations, but no less trepidation about speaking to these challenging topics.

While our society is slowly changing, many of our companies are still run by white, upper- or middle-class, middle-aged, heterosexual men. Nonprofits can be more diverse, but it's incorrect to assume that simply having a more diverse employee base means that these important power currents aren't at work, or that they are easy to talk about.

Fear of Rejection

A particularly raw emotion, fear of rejection confuses discussions of nonprofit power and stymies decision-making. According to author and therapist, John Amodeo, Ph.D.[5], "... fear of rejection is one of the deepest human fears. Biologically, we're wired with a longing to belong; we fear being seen in a critical way. We're anxious about the prospect of being cut off, demeaned, or isolated. We fear being alone."

While being rejected by family or friends can have a devastating effect on an individual, so can exclusion from an organization. This is particularly concerning for people outside the dominant white culture. People with differences experience this fear even more acutely.

In our observations, people who work in nonprofits are consistently loyal to their organizations and committed to their mission. None of them wants to be seen as uncommitted; many are personally drawn to the mission of their organization and have a deep and personal relationship with the communities they are engaged to serve. What's

---

5 PsychCentral.com, *Deconstructing Fear of Rejection: What Are We Really Afraid Of?*

more, they are willing to stay in untenable situations in order to be faithful to and advance the needs of their constituents.

This tenacity and faithfulness often makes people hesitant to bring up the uncomfortable topics that may cause them to be ostracized. The potential loss of affiliation is too great. Fear of rejection limits the issues that people are willing to discuss, and thus for many people, realigning power and decision-making in their organization can feel too risky.

Now consider what you know about your own organization, and think about your answers to the following questions:

- ❖ Do you have a method for talking about power and decision-making in your organization?

- ❖ Do you have a language that helps you navigate the worries that spring up when you assert your claim to the decisions you want to make?

- ❖ Do you know how to talk about decision-making without inciting low-level fear in yourself or other people?

- ❖ Do you know how to speak up and advocate for the decisions you want to make?

If you answered yes to any of the above, you are unusual—in a good way!. Unfortunately, most organizations don't share a common language for talking about the power inherent in decision-making, or the fear that it creates.

THE SECOND SURPRISE

The truth is, most people don't know how to *think* holistically about decision-making in their organizations, and they certainly don't know how to *talk* about it. And because they don't know how to think or talk about it, most people assume there's nothing they can do to alter these unhealthy patterns in their organization, so they simply accept the inefficient processes they have.

THIS IS THE SECOND SURPRISE ABOUT POWER AND DECISION-MAKING:

Because creating change is a high-stakes activity,
it requires a shared language for talking about it and
a methodology for thinking about it.

This language needs to make roles and responsibilities clear and allow everyone to manage the power-related emotions that lurk in the shadows. Without a language for talking about these topics, it's difficult to address what's working, what's not working, and what to do about it.

But language alone is not enough; it must coincide with a methodology. A process to deliver clarity and insight—that is, a structured way to evaluate and prioritize decisions, and a framework for figuring out who in the organization is best suited to make the decisions at hand—must be available to all.

Let's revisit the process issue from earlier. Knowing that nonprofit leadership is challenging, and that most leaders cannot magically manufacture money or time (or a board that heeds their every wish), how do leaders leverage their existing resources? How do they improve the bonds between staff, save time and money, and allow the mission of the organization to be optimally served?

By definition, the answer points to, you guessed it: decision-making. Getting clear about which decisions should be a priority to your organization (and which should not) allows everyone involved to save time by focusing on the things that matter most.

If we asked you, "Do you understand how decision-making works in your organization?" it's likely you would say yes, and then go on to describe a way of doing things that works some of the time, but still leaves certain people overwhelmed, and other people frustrated. In doing so, you've just described your decision-making ecosystem (more on that later), which has been around since the dawn of your organization.

Take a moment to reflect on how decisions get made in your organization by considering the following:

- ❖ How would you describe the process to an outsider?

- ❖ Is it effective or ineffective?

- ❖ Is it too speedy or too slow?

- ❖ Do you spend a lot of time trying to figure out who will make what decisions?

- ❖ Do you revisit decisions you've previously made?

With these observations in mind, write a brief description below of your existing system.

THE THIRD SURPRISE

When we ask the question, "Do you have a process for decision-making in your organization that is clear, that everyone understands and can talk about, that manages risk, and that can be taught and implemented without awkwardness or discomfort?" most executive directors would say no.

This may shock you as these are smart and committed people; they know what they want to achieve. In fact, all executive directors we've talked to can speak with clarity and authenticity about where they would like the organization to be in five years. And many we've polled and worked with would be willing to divest themselves of a portion of their decision-making authority, if they had a clear process for taking that step. They are also willing to revise the scope of their decision-making, if they can be assured that nothing will fall through the cracks. In short, they are often willing to change, but they simply don't have a ready-made solution.

THIS IS THE THIRD SURPRISE ABOUT POWER AND DECISION-MAKING:

It's vital to an organization's success, but most leaders don't see decision-making as an opportunity for growth until they are shown a way to think about it, and taught a hands-on way to do it, that is feasible and makes sense.

You may be surprised to learn that getting clear on power and decision-making is actually not time-consuming or especially difficult. It's "low-hanging fruit" that can be implemented quickly to set expectations, gain focus, and generate quick results.

Understanding who in the organization can make the decision (*besides* the executive director) allows staff to use their knowledge, talents, and energies to serve the organization better, and it frees up the leadership to attend to activities that support the larger mission. And knowing how to advocate for decision-making, and how to create a unified decision-making *team*, allows an organization to manage the risks of important decisions, while moving quickly to address real program needs.

In sum, we believe it's possible to talk about power and decision-making without stirring up a hornet's nest in your organization. We believe it's also possible to give away this power to others without creating organizational chaos or weakening the roles of the executive director or the board. Stay tuned ... we're going to teach you how, but first let's take a look at how the roles of power and decision-making are thought of and executed in your organization.

KEY TAKEAWAYS

Decision-making is an act of power, and it often provokes fear.

With such significant societal and personal pressures in evidence, executive directors and their teams fear failure.

Significant changes to the power and decision-making practices of nonprofits must be led by the people who currently have influence and make decisions.

Creating change is a high-stakes activity that requires a shared language and methodology. Without this, people may resist decision-making opportunities because they are too afraid to engage.

Nonprofit leaders tend to take on too many responsibilities and weigh in on too many decisions, which can hamper and elongate the process.

Most leaders don't see decision-making as an opportunity for growth until they are shown a way to think about it, and taught a hands-on way to do it, that is feasible and makes sense.

Fear of failure, fear of rejection, and fear of conflict often create unhealthy practices that stymie organizations.

Leaders are often willing to divest themselves of decision-making authority to be able to focus more and face less exhaustion, if they have a framework for doing so.

Left to current practices, someone will eventually make a decision, but imagine how much more successful you could be if you decided in advance who was going to make (or support) the important decisions in your organization.

2

UNDERSTANDING THE ROLES
OF POWER AND DECISION-MAKING

This chapter is directed primarily at people who currently have organizational power, so if you're the executive director, in senior leadership, or a member of the board, this chapter will speak specifically to you. However, even if you're not in one of these roles right now, I encourage you to read on to learn more about the issues and challenges these leaders face—and that you may one day face should you be promoted—and how their conscious and unconscious views on power affect your job. I also invite you to take a moment to consider your own views on power and decision-making, and how they may differ from those in authority.

Whether you have taken the time to reflect on it or not, you have either created or inherited a power and decision-making model in your organization, and your daily actions reinforce that model. While new and current employees learn by listening and watching, and thereby discern indirectly what level of decisions they can or can't make, rarely is this topic ever diagrammed or explicitly discussed. In short, these team members are left to merely sense whether it's safe to make decisions in your environment, or whether they should defer.

Individuals who are somewhat bold may make certain assumptions and plow forward, but this does not always work. We've all seen leaders and staff make the critical mistake of acting without understanding the norms of their new nonprofit, and are then never able to recover from the resulting confusion and conflict.

As most new employees will hold back and take in their environment before attempting to assert themselves, they will nonetheless take note if they see disconnects between how the organization talks and what actually happens. Organization charts are helpful, but they almost never reflect how power and decision-making are actually pursued in an organization. For example, people may have senior titles, but this does not mean they are making the crucial decisions in your organization; in fact, their actual responsibilities may not be reflective of their grade at all.

Be aware that no one is going to come out and ask you for your views on this topic. Why? Because it can feel too risky. As we've said, rarely do people have the language or a framework for raising this topic, so your actions are observed as a measure of "how things are," and the beliefs that underlie these actions are rarely questioned, lurking like an iceberg below the surface.

THE ICEBERG

If you lead a nonprofit, your beliefs about power and decision-making are already "in the water" of your environment. Even if you haven't talked about them, rest assured your beliefs are well known in your organization, and that they influence your staff and your board. Think about it: Do your employees seem to instinctively know which decisions you want to make? Or, from another perspective, are you frustrated because your staff and/or your board have little interest in making decisions? Either way, it's important to realize you've trained them through your actions.

Executive directors and their senior leadership are often asked to be the default decision-makers on the most crucial organizational, programmatic, and fundraising decisions. And this structure is *implicit*. If you don't initiate an *explicit* conversation about this, your team and your board are unlikely to bring up these topics. Everyone will assume they already know where power and decision-making exist, yet when questioned, they may or may not actually know what you want.

And the situation becomes even more complicated if you've come to leadership after the original executive director has left. If this is the case, then to at least some extent you have inherited the effects of your predecessor's beliefs and assumptions about power and decision-making. Even the smartest executive directors may labor for years encountering curious resistance before they truly understand the parameters of this inherited system.

X Marks the Spot
How transparent is your organizational decision-making?

Completely Transparent

Somewhat Clear

Murky

Completely Hidden

Organizations can be slow to change in this arena, especially when the topic isn't addressed head-on. The point here is that your beliefs as a leader have a powerful influence on what happens in your organization, and not examining what is true for you doesn't make the iceberg go away; it merely continues to make the whole structure more difficult to see.

YOUR PERSONAL INFLUENCES

With regard to decision-making, everyone has a different take, and there isn't one universal answer. What's consistent, however, is that each person's views on power and decision-making are unique and quite personal, having been shaped by their earliest interactions within their families and then refined by their work and life experiences.

To determine *your* particular style in this arena, here are some questions for you to consider. Write your answers in the space provided.

1. Who in your family are you most similar to in terms of how you use power and make decisions? Why?

2. Who in your family are you least similar to? Why?

3. Who in your career has had the most influence on your thoughts on power and decision-making, either positively or negatively? Why?

4. What messages and lessons have you absorbed from these people and your experiences with them?

5. How does this perspective inform how you wield power and make decisions in your organization?

6. In your current organization, what power do you assume to be yours and what decisions do you make?

7. What power and decision-making responsibilities reside with your board?

8. What power and decision-making responsibilities reside with your leadership team?

9. What power and decision-making authority do members of your staff hold?

10. How much have you spoken to your organization about your personal views on power and decision-making?

11. Have you tried to create a power and decision-making philosophy for your organization?

12. What power and decision-making authority have you given to others? How did you make the assessment that these individuals were qualified?

13. What do you do when you're disappointed in the decision-making capabilities and outcomes of others?

14. Do you have the decision-making focus you need to do your job effectively, or are you making too many decisions?

15. Can you give explicit decision-making authority to others and feel good about it?

16. What biases do you have about who should have decision-making power in your organization?

Think about these questions honestly—there are no right or wrong answers, and there is no rating scale. It's simply important to think about these issues and to become comfortable revealing your answers to yourself (and eventually to people you work with). And don't be afraid to ask other people on your team the same questions to get their perspective. You may hear something surprising and informative; perhaps what you'll learn will differ from what you've assumed to be true. Either way, it will enable you to broach this topic again with more ease.

FOUR MODELS OF DYSFUNCTIONAL NONPROFIT POWER AND DECISION-MAKING

In our work with nonprofits, we typically see four dysfunctional decision-making models. In some organizations, one model is clearly dominant; in others, there's a mixture of approaches. But organizations don't easily transition from one model to another. They find one that works and stay with it until a crisis changes the dynamic—or until someone teaches them a new and better way to organize and do things.

Within the established hierarchies of nonprofits—the board that provides overarching governance; the executive director or CEO who establishes strategic insights, creates plans, and provides day-to-day supervision; a leadership team, if the organization is big enough; and unless it's an organization of one person, a multiple-person staff—the members don't use power and make decisions in the same way. This being true, we've observed four general power and decision-making cultures in nonprofits that have dysfunctional elements.

FOUR DYSFUNCTIONAL DECISION-MAKING MODELS

1. My Way or The Highway	(Concentrated)
2. Don't Make Me Come in There	(Unresolved)
3. We're All in This Together	(Consensus)
4. You Can Do It	(Delegation)

1. The "My-Way-or-the-Highway" Decision-Making Model (Concentrated)

In the My-Way-or-the-Highway culture, power and decision-making are concentrated in the hands of a disproportionately small number of people. In this environment, the executive director or a small cadre of leaders may make all the important decisions. The motivation behind this is clear: fear of failure. There is too much perceived to be at stake to risk making a bad decision.

This feeling also can be exacerbated if the leader has a particular set of beliefs and biases about who in the organization is qualified to make a decision—especially when those biases are linked to whether or not someone is different from the leader with respect to age, race, gender, class, and sexual orientation. Sometimes these biases also include education; people who have a shared educational background can erroneously believe that people from their alma mater or a similar one are more capable than others.

In these organizations, anyone not in the inner circle is essentially considered an "implementer." In this formulation, you will often find a vice president and director-level staff who have comparatively little power and decision-making authority. They are being paid as if they were decision-makers but are given little opportunity to weigh in on and make important decisions.

In this culture, the staff knows that decision-making is held tight, and they rarely dissent openly. As such, the executive director is always the default decision-maker. If the staff is puzzled about what course to take, the standard practice is to ask their leader. When offered the chance to advocate for decision-making authority, the staff typically defers to the executive director—even if pushed to advocate.

Organizations with a My-Way-or-the-Highway decision-making culture can be slow to respond to pressing decisions, because so many of them have to go through the executive director. This creates bottlenecks that slow progress, resulting in the organization not fully utilizing the decision-making skills of their employees.

This culture is authoritarian by nature, but sometimes leaders want to hide the level of concentrated decision-making they possess. In this case, the executive director will mask her or his ultimate power under the guise of protracted collaboration, typically calling a meeting with the pertinent staff, mindful of the decision s/he wants to make, and then "gently" steering the conversation and the team to her or his conclusion.

A practitioner of this model—an experienced executive director—once told us, "I'm really making the decision, but I don't want them to know that." We see this often in people who have founded organizations or have run them for many years. In this situation, the leaders claim explicit and implicit decision-making "rights" simply because of their long-held position—and staff continue to defer to their perspective.

While favoring high standards of control and decision-making certainty, this model does not involve the full capacities of the organization. As a result, staff is essentially prohibited from taking on increased decision-making power.

2. The "Don't-Make-Me-Come-in-There" Decision-Making Model (Unresolved)

In the Don't-Make-Me-Come-in-There culture, power and decision-making are characterized by friction because there is no set standard, and the organization has a cultural bias to avoid conflict. Power may be shared, but it is often unresolved; by the time people actually talk to each other, resentment and defensiveness have been allowed to build up, such that getting to the bottom of issues becomes difficult. The status quo is then allowed to persist, causing unending friction that may show up as disagreement among the team members about the mission of the organization, the delivery of services, or any number of other issues.

In this situation, low-level friction always exists, but its effect on decision-making isn't talked about openly. The executive director holds the belief that "You should just be able to get along," and s/he reinforces this belief by staying hands-off until there's a crisis. Team members subsequently develop a learned attitude of "fend for yourself" that often sounds like, "I don't trust that we can come up with a good solution, so I'm going to do whatever I want— even if I know it's less than optimal." This approach allows the whole organization to make sporadic leaps forward, but not necessarily in planned or coordinated ways.

In larger organizations, we see unresolved power and decision-making dynamics between groups, one of the most common being between regional and national operations, but numerous others can feel in perpetual conflict. Talking about this conflict or resolving it means creating boundaries and agreements, while *not* talking about it creates the illusion of freedom to do what one wants, and thus the conflict persists. This tension does little to advance the mission of the organization, because the fear of talking about conflict prevents effective discussions of power and decision-making.

Bottlenecks are created here as well, because decisions lie unresolved for months or even years. As people become invested in their polarity, little is done to resolve these outstanding power struggles. And because the executive director or senior leadership does not want to give preferential treatment to one group over the other, the two groups continue to flounder. At some point, the executive director may weigh in, and then, after a good deal of conflict, issue an edict that usually disappoints both sides.

In this model, staff can—and often try to—advocate for increased decision-making, but there isn't an established mechanism for doing so. Both sides appeal to the executive director or some other member of the organization's inner circle because they feel powerless to resolve this situation between themselves.

3. "We're-All-in-This-Together" Decision-Making Model (Consensus)

In the We're-All-in-This-Together model, power and decision-making are assumed to be the province of the group. Underpinning this model is a desire to avoid conflict, but also an urge to involve all the relevant parties. While the inclusion of all who have a stake in the decision is laudable, the weakness of the model is that it usually leads to a great deal of talk and no clear path to decision-making. Worse yet, while good decisions can come from this approach, it's not clear to the group how to manage it well. Sometimes, the involvement of the parties does lead to a good outcome, but just as easily, the decisions that come from consensus decision-making are the amalgamation of

competing agendas. Elegant, streamlined solutions are not often the outcome of this method.

The prevailing attitude of this model is "We need everyone's buy-in. We have to decide together," which in truth is quite prevalent in nonprofits. One theory as to why consensus models persist is that many nonprofits want to reject the hierarchical, command-and-control models that are common in for-profit organizations. They perceive the for-profit model as perhaps efficient, but focused more on profits than on people, and therefore want to do something different. In reaction, as we've mentioned, many nonprofits operate in a familial organizational structure. Everyone is part of the family and no one wants to risk working outside of the family's decision-making norm or to harm the cohesion of the group. As such, the We're-All-in-This-Together model enables people to state their views and argue for their positions without upsetting "the family." Maintaining the family unit sometimes eclipses the urgency and importance of the decision that needs to be made.

And how *do* decisions get made using this model? Sometimes the stronger participants push their agendas for group approval. In this scenario, the more powerful members of the team repeatedly assert their perspective, slowly grinding down other opposing thoughts. The people who pursue this approach won't necessarily ask to make the decision, but they will push hard to make their solution the only surviving option. Sometimes competing options are put to a vote, while other times teams are forced to make a decision by sheer exhaustion ("I don't want to talk about it anymore, let's decide") or by pointing to the calendar ("We can't spend any more time talking about it. We have to act").

The We're-All-in-This-Together model assumes an altruistic view of power and decision-making, which subtly condemns the overt use of power and condones unclear decision-making processes. In the altruistic view, the prevailing assumption is that everyone is doing his or her best, and that people make rational decisions to advance the mission. Under altruistic philosophy, consensus decision-making enables the team to avoid conflict that may threaten the safety of the group; when these decisions go wrong, the group finesses who was responsible. Using this method, team cohesion is maintained and conflict is limited, but clear discussions about power and decision-making are also avoided.

4. "You-Can-Do-It!" Decision-Making Model (Delegation)

Occasionally, we see leaders and organizations that have consciously worked hard to delegate decision-making in their organizations. Using participative management techniques, they have taken an active role in delegating decisions to more people, and while delegation is a positive step forward, this model suffers from several inherent weaknesses.

In a delegation environment, power and decision-making are usually given to a less experienced person by a more senior person. There is often some discussion that ensues about the importance of the decision being granted and a symbolic hand-off; however, rarely is the less-experienced person allowed to say no, and even more rarely is this person given an opportunity to advocate to make more decisions or different ones.

Depending on the personality and experience of the subordinate, s/he may move quickly forward or may hesitate because of being in new or uncertain territory. The subordinate may not feel comfortable making the decision s/he has been given (or may not have much interest in the decision itself).

In the You-Can-Do-It model, it is also not clear whether the senior person will really surrender the decision and let go. If this person subtly or more specifically reasserts her or his claim to the decision, the subordinate will usually back off. This is particularly true in nonprofits where people strive to minimize conflict.

In each of these models, you will see some benefits and some drawbacks:

❖ In the **My-Way-or-the-Highway**—or *concentrated*—model, you may get efficiency but sacrifice participation.

❖ In the **Don't-Make-Me-Come-in-There**—or *unresolved*—model, you may avoid conflict but sacrifice clarity and optimal solutions.

❖ In the **We're-All-in-This-Together**—or *consensus*—model, you may get participation but sacrifice innovation.

❖ In the **You-Can-Do-It**—or *delegation*—model, you may get participation but will put engagement in a prescribed and limited box.

These aren't the only models that can exist, of course. But they are the common ones —and they are all dysfunctional in different ways. In later chapters of this book, we will talk in detail about how the Decision Clarity model works to alleviate the drawbacks of each of these frameworks, as well as how it allows your organization to become more agile and functional. But for now, let's keep the focus on exploring the current method of power and decision-making in your own organization.

WHAT DECISION-MAKING MODEL DOES YOUR ORGANIZATION USE?

In our work with nonprofits, we meet many extraordinary people. Every day, we encounter individuals with a single-minded passion to make a difference in the world. While each person comes to us with a specialized set of skills and a unique personality, it's striking how similar their experiences are when it comes to power and decision-making in their organizations.

Time and time again, we hear the same frustrations: lack of progress on fundamental goals, festering conflict, stymied growth, staff churn, employee dissatisfaction, and executive director burnout. All of these issues are a result of ineffective views on who has power, and who can make what decisions.

You may or may not recognize yourself in the statements on the following page, but take a moment to consider how you might answer the following two questions:

1. If you could fly over your organization and observe how decisions are made, what would you see?

2. Who has power in your organization and who doesn't?

In 2014, we did an online survey and asked these questions (and a host of others); the respondents were executive directors, board members, and nonprofit staff. Fifty people responded, and many were motivated to write lengthy answers. Take a look at a small sample of what they had to say.

QUESTION 1:

If you could fly over your organization and observe how decisions are made, what would you see?

"You would see lots of meetings and huddles. We work mostly based on consensus. There is lots of opportunity for the team to give feedback."

"I would have to fly over the organization at night once a month during board meetings to see any real decisions being made."

"Underneath the practical, everyday sorts of meetings and decisions is a layer of behind-the-scenes decision-making that a flyover would miss. These meetings are held between two or three people, outside of 'public' view, over dinner, or in private. These conversations are of a more political nature, and they create the relationships that allow for other decisions to actually happen."

"You'd see the executive director making all the final decisions. He attempts to empower the rest of the staff to make decisions; however, the culture and the vibe in the office still lead us to consult with him before making final decisions."

"I would see pockets of people working in silos with no transparency around decision-making, and people who are burned out by our mission."

"With the organization of which I am a founder and board member, all the decisions are made by majority consensus. However, for truly important decisions, we require a 100% agreement in order to move forward."

"I would see a pyramid, with the president on the top, the other elected officers below him (vice president, treasurer, secretary), then the appointed positions on the bottom (committee leads)."

What is striking in all these comments is that people working in nonprofits are quite savvy as to how their decision-making structures work, where power resides, and whether the status quo is effective or not. But while they're aware of how the structures of their organization function, they have no idea how to (or whether they can) talk about them publicly, or how to change them for the better.

QUESTION 2:

Who has power in your organization and who doesn't?

"The one in power usually sends out an email discussing operating procedures and giving us an update on the current status of the organization."

"If you have the higher title, you beat out anyone lower down based on the title alone, not on the merits of your (or anyone else's) ideas/abilities."

"Direct service providers from my experience are listened to because we do the groundwork; however, we typically don't have a huge voice in the overall policymaking process of the organization. People with the least amount of power tend to be "peer" educators or outreach workers who come from the community we're serving. Education level also plays into who has power and who does not."

"I think the people without power were generally less connected to the ear of the executive director. We had one woman who was fairly outspoken and overpowering and was very friendly with the executive director. She ended up having a lot of influence but didn't really represent the agency and what we stood for."

"I look to see who makes the decisions, and who often ends up stalling things."

"Board members who have children in the program (adult day-care program) have more power than those who don't. These people make decisions based on what they think will be best for their individual child, not the program as a whole."

"Staff who work on the floor on a daily basis often have great ideas, but aren't given the chance to share them because they are considered to be too low on the corporate ladder. Most of those in power have their power because they contributed to the organization and bought their positions."

"Men who have been a part of the organization the longest hold the greatest power. Those who are perceived by these men to not have the "old-school solidarity" or spirit aren't given much agency. Although some newer staff has risen (over many years) in decision-making positions, their choices are ultimately steered by the old-guard males who run the organization. The executive director is a woman. She has some power but is realistically controlled by the men too."

You may notice that these quotes are not particularly positive. As a leader, this may trouble you as you begin to consider what the people in your own organization might say. Rest assured, you won't be alone if the thought of talking about power and decision-making makes you nervous, especially without a standardized way of discussing it. Again, part of the power of Decision Clarity is that it offers a language for talking about these topics openly and without fear, which we will give guidance on in various areas of upcoming chapters.

In the space provided on the next page, describe your decision-making model. Pay special attention to where it works and where it doesn't, considering the following questions:

- ❖ If you look at the models articulated earlier in this chapter, which most closely resembles your organization?

- ❖ How often does your organization practice some form of *concentrated, unresolved, consensus,* or *delegation* decision-making?

- ❖ Is there some other model at play in your nonprofit? How does it work? What might you call it?

What Are the Costs and Benefits of Your Model?

In the space provided, list the top three costs and benefits of your decision-making model.

Costs	Benefits
1.	1.
2.	2.
3.	3.

In organizations that use *concentrated* decision-making, we often see a level of passiveness and learned helplessness in the staff, who are taught through trial and error that their efforts often don't matter (or will be undermined); as a result, they don't trust that the situation will ever be different.

In organizations that practice *unresolved* and *consensus* decision-making, passive-aggressiveness is common. Participating in this behavior allows each person to test the decision-making waters to see how much room they have to participate, without necessarily staking a claim one way or another. In these organizations, staff doesn't trust that they will be able to participate safely without repercussions; for all the warm feelings that emanate from nonprofits, trust is often lacking in these organizations. Ultimately, fear of failure inhibits trust and prevents real engagement.

In organizations that practice *delegation*, a form of learned helplessness is common. People wait to be told what they can do; they don't offer up solutions for fear of overstepping some unseen boundary.

Take a moment to consider how trust operates in your organization, given your current model of decision-making.

- Do you see your staff as hesitant to make decisions?

- If they make decisions, how often are these decisions overruled?

- Are too many decisions made by too many people?

- Do people wait to be told what they can decide?

SELF-LIMITING BELIEFS ABOUT POWER

Many who work in nonprofits share some deeply ingrained habits and attitudes. Some have been studied and written about, but others can be invisible to the naked eye if they aren't called out and addressed. More importantly, when these behaviors and attitudes form the unseen bedrock of a nonprofit organization, they add another dimension to what makes power and decision-making so difficult to talk about.

In this section, we will take a hard look at these beliefs and examine both the behaviors that result from them and their effectiveness. You may or may not fall victim to these, but they are prevalent in the nonprofit sector, and they limit our collective ability to create clear and effective decision-making practices.

Because we don't want them to silently impede your ability to implement the Decision Clarity method, it's important to call these beliefs out now; you can think of the following as your secret weapon as you embark on clarifying the processes in your organization. The content here will show you where some of the hidden obstacles are so that you can spot them quickly and overcome them with grace and ease.

World View

Let's start with the concepts of kindness, gratitude, deference, and dependence, and what happens when people in nonprofits unconsciously take these to an extreme. If this sounds outrageous, consider the following questions:

1. What do you do when people you feel indebted to bring you suggestions and ideas that are so off track that you find yourself speechless?

2. What do you say if their ideas are good, but you already have a focus you're pursuing?

3. Does your gratitude for past support overly influence how you respond to your supporters?

4. When people in your organization bring up an ill-advised objective or a flawed strategy, do you kindly acknowledge what s/he has said and move on? Or do you spend more time than is really necessary vetting an idea that you know is off target?

5. When people don't perform well, are you clear with them about their performance, or do you sweep your disappointment under the rug? Do you tend to be more kind, or more truthful?

6. When board members fail to come to meetings, raise money, or even provide feedback, are you kind and understanding? Do you speak to the infraction, or feel so grateful to the people on the board that you'll take any morsel of help that is offered?

7. If you're a member of a minority community, do you offer too much deference and gratitude in order to not be perceived as ungrateful, overstepping, or arrogant?

8. If you're managing people who have different levels of privilege, are you aware of your biases and how they may influence your ability to engage your team honestly and completely?

If you found yourself slightly uncomfortable reading these questions, you're not alone. All of them point to an underlying set of attitudes about what is allowed and what isn't. You can think of these attitudes as a psychological framework of sorts, one that reinforces a collective worldview that then acts to drive behavior. In short, these beliefs dictate what you believe you can say and do.

Beliefs and Results

Let's start with some central beliefs that permeate nonprofit culture:

BELIEF #1: We must always be "kind" to our supporters.

BELIEF #2: We must always be "grateful" to our supporters.

BELIEF #3: We must always "listen with deference" to our supporters.

BELIEF #4: We are "dependent" on our supporters, so we must never upset them.

Again, the goal here is not to shock or upset anyone, but to highlight some attitudes that can work against your goals and plans when they are taken to an extreme. We aren't telling you to be "unkind" or "ungrateful" or to "not listen" or to be so "independent" that you're on an island unto yourself; there simply needs to be a balance.

In contrast to the need for balance, we see varieties of not telling the truth (silence, hedging, placating, obfuscating, or not being direct), as well as not feeling the right to demand or push, and not being able to say "no." When these good and natural reactions become extreme, they inhibit people and render them less powerful—and less capable decision-makers.

Let's look at each belief and how it can affect power and decision-making in nonprofits.

Belief #1:

We must always be "kind" to our supporters.

In her *Chronicle of Philanthropy* article[6], reporter Caroline Preston challenges this first belief by quoting Albert Ruesga, president of the Greater New Orleans Foundation:

> ... The culture of overweening politeness in American philanthropy is leading to our ruin. It keeps me from telling you, in the clearest possible terms, that your five-year, $2-million initiative to end homelessness is well-intentioned, magical thinking at best and bone-headed ignorance at worst.

Ruesga goes on to state that:

> ... when people are so worried about offending each other that they don't engage in honest debate, that can cause poor grant-making practices to perpetuate, silly projects to be started, and weak leaders to remain in their jobs too long.

Vignetta Charles, senior vice president of AIDS United, was also interviewed for the article, and her take on how kindness gets in the way of nonprofit progress was just as direct. "It's harder for us to talk about this in philanthropy than in the corporate world because we've had this genteel attitude," she says. "We've been too nice to each other for too long."

Emmett Carson, president of the Silicon Valley Community Foundation, weighed in with his stance that even though he encourages nonprofit people to be direct, "... it's

---

[6] "Some Nonprofit Leaders Ask: Is Philanthropy Killing Itself With Kindness?" *Chronicle of Philanthropy,* February 2013.

difficult for many people to feel comfortable doing so. People don't choose nonprofit jobs for the pay, so the work itself becomes more important. Aware that their colleagues are making personal sacrifices, charity and foundation workers may be reluctant to point out each other's shortcomings."

The key suggestions offered by the author and the nonprofit individuals she interviewed include:

❖ an increased focus on results rather than intention

❖ more direct feedback in the face of failure

❖ tougher, more focused, and results-driven boards that are less "celebratory and deferential"

All of these "kindness reduction" efforts would benefit nonprofit operations, and it's likely you see these kindness dynamics at play in your organization, only you haven't thought to question them. To be clear, we aren't challenging the need to be kind to those in need or who support the work of nonprofits. Still, the need for kindness is not an either/or proposition. It's possible to be kind—and respectful—and say what needs to be said.

How do you, personally, balance this tension? To discover where you fall on the scales of kindness and truth, try picturing how you communicate with one of your key supporters.

Kindness

❖ When you interact with this supporter, where do you typically fall on the "kindness" scale below?

1	2	3	4	5
(a little)		(balanced)		(too much)

Telling the Truth

❖ Are you straightforward with this supporter, or do you fall back on a "genteel" attitude?

❖ Where are you on the truth scale?

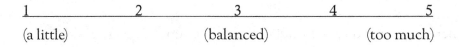

1   2   3   4   5

(a little)   (balanced)   (too much)

Take a moment to think about how you feel about your answers.

Belief #2:

We must always be "grateful" to our supporters.

There is nothing wrong with being grateful; it's an essential characteristic for humans and organizations. But what we've seen is that if a nonprofit receiving assistance perceives itself as either financially, politically, or programmatically weak, it will often act excessively grateful for any support. Most nonprofits have one or more of the above weaknesses, which affects their sense of power and decision-making.

We know that nonprofits are not often in a position of financial strength. According to The National Center on Charitable Statistics, at the end of 2013 there were 1,409,430 registered nonprofit organizations in the United States. Of that number, 1,032,285—or 73%—had operating budgets of $1 million or less. Smaller organizations have fewer resources, and this tends to make them feel less powerful—and more "grateful."

Look at the gratitude and power lines that follow.

Gratitude

❖ Thinking of one of your benefactors, how would you rate your degree of gratitude?

1	2	3	4	5
(a little)		(balanced)		(too much)

Where does your organization fall? Are you in the zone of optimal (balanced) gratitude or do you let excessive gratitude impact your organization?

Power

❖ Considering that same benefactor, how powerful do you feel when interacting with this person?

1	2	3	4	5
(a little)		(balanced)		(too much)

Have you seen examples of how excessive gratitude and little power have created challenges for you or your organization?

Take a moment to think about how you feel about your answers.

While we hesitate to compare for-profits to nonprofits, for-profit organizations do have one inherent advantage: they attract investors, employees, and customers who want to be connected to a particular enterprise. Put another way, people seek to be connected with companies and products for intellectual, financial, or ego reasons. And the nature of the financial exchange is clear: "I'm going to buy something, and you will provide me with a product or service," or "I'm going to join your company, and you will pay me a competitive salary and benefits," or "I'm going to invest in your company and expect to make money." If these transactions fail to be beneficial, people walk away from them and look for another opportunity.

In the nonprofit world, the natural exchange is not as clear. Rather than being a financial transaction, the exchange is considered a gift—and with gifts, there are different dynamics at play. This is why board members arrive late to meetings or don't show up at all: their service is a gift. This is also why funders feel they have the right to make demands and why people who work for nonprofits feel that their work is "never enough." The nature of the exchange isn't clear, and there is no definitive "end" to the relationship.

People in nonprofits feel beholden to everyone in their environment. Demonstrating gratitude to your constituencies is your way of paying them back for their contributions, and gratitude *in moderation* is always a good thing. But excessive gratitude, particularly when it shows up as staff not feeling they have a right to demand, criticize, or push, can be destructive to your organization.

The primary problem is this: when people and organizations have limited power to influence their environments, they rarely flourish. Hence, when nonprofits feel powerless and at the mercy of their supporters, it permeates the organization at an unspoken level, affecting the organizational and individual views of how one wields power, and of how decisions are made in the organization and by whom.

Belief #3:

We must always "listen with deference" to our supporters.

We all know that listening is a positive skill; there's much to be gained by being a good listener. *If you listen, you will likely increase your understanding. If you listen, you will connect better with people. If you listen, you will gain the respect of others.* But listening without setting expectations is counterproductive, and it gives the impression that you'll take action when that may not be your intention. When we're "too kind," we mask the truth. When we're "too grateful," we forsake our own power. If we listen, but don't set expectations, we risk being unfaithful to ourselves and to the person to whom we're listening.

In 2013, we performed a Decision Clarity engagement with Jill Ellis and her leadership team at the Center for Early Intervention on Deafness (CEID) in Berkeley, California, an organization that provides services for young children from birth to age five who are deaf, hard of hearing, or have severe speech and language delays. Jill was one of CEID's co-founders in 1980 and the original executive director.

During a one-on-one session with Jill, she confessed that she often felt over-whelmed by the number of ideas, suggestions, and demands from her constituents. That morning, one of her parents came to her office to suggest another program change. Jill listened to this person and agreed that the idea had merit. In our conversation she recounted this interaction, and with resignation and disappointment she sighed and said, "I'll just add this good idea to the list of things that will never get done. I simply don't have the time or resources to make this happen."

Jill's experience is not unusual. Part of the issue is that people who work in nonprofits live in a "suggestion culture." Supporters believe they have the ability and the right to offer a suggestion, make a demand, or pose a question at any time, and they have the expectation that it will be dealt with expeditiously. It's an unspoken expectation that often goes unchallenged, resulting in bitterness, confusion, and resentment if the suggestion or request isn't acted upon.

When dealing with supporters, listening without setting expectations is dangerous, and yet we see it as a common nonprofit practice. So what's at the heart of this listening challenge? The reluctance to say "no." Nonprofit leaders don't feel they have the power to take that stance. They fear alienating a key individual, making it difficult for them to reconcile the very real challenges before them and their own limitations. Some leaders think if they say "no," they won't be doing everything in their power to address the needs that their nonprofit is supposed to meet. The result is that they're essentially caught in a form of cognitive dissonance where they are challenged by the conflicting beliefs that they're "good people" and that "good people" don't say "no."

Belief #4:

We are "dependent" on our supporters, so we must never upset them.

This last belief sums it all up while boiling it down to the one emotion that is always lurking in the corner: fear. As we discussed in Chapter 1, fear of failure, conflict, and rejection drive the four beliefs highlighted here, and excessive kindness, gratitude, and deference are the byproducts of these fears. As we know from Lord Acton, "Power corrupts, and absolute power corrupts absolutely." When we fear our own power, it destroys our ability to change the world, it hides the truth and our ability to act on it, and it ruins effective decision-making.

To put it directly, people are driven to extremes of being kind, grateful, and deferent because they feel dependent and vulnerable. This excessiveness can be ruinous if it goes unchallenged. When people working in nonprofits feel too dependent, their views of their own power get skewed, warping their ability to make decisions. And even if this is a reflection of an underlying reality (and not just fear), *believing* in this asymmetrical structure of power erodes people's sense of what they can accomplish and how their organization can behave.

ANTIDOTES TO FEAR-BASED BELIEFS AND BEHAVIORS

Now that we've teased this out, let's talk about the steps you can take to address these beliefs and not succumb to the behaviors that come from fear. These steps will prepare you for the Decision Clarity activities in Part II of this book. Please know that while it's not likely that the suggestions below will eliminate *all* your fears, they will certainly better prepare you to do the activities to come.

Following are four antidotes to the beliefs and behaviors we've just talked about. Consider these suggestions as small steps in an important direction.

1. Calmly bring up uncomfortable topics that no one else wants to broach.

When you can bring up topics that everyone typically avoids, you are claiming your power. Why? Because there's influence afforded to the person who is willing to bring up the difficult subjects no one else wants to touch. It sounds obvious, but it's easier to assert more control of the situation if you bring up the tough issues of your own volition rather than if you wait for them to explode. Be the person in your environment who is willing to have the hard conversations.

You'll feel more powerful and you'll garner the respect of your colleagues. What's more, if you take this step, you'll tacitly give others permission to do so too.

Here's some language you can use:

"I want to talk with you about this challenging issue. I need_____. Can you help me?" Or, "I want to take the following action: _____. Do I have your support?"

It really is that simple. Delaying and deferring only lead to problems, so be the first to speak up and you'll be able to more effectively guide the emerging process and take a leadership role in the solution.

2. Tell the truth.

Don't be "kind" if kindness obfuscates the truth. When you simply tell the truth, it's easier on everyone, more effective, and kinder than avoidance. And people actually want it. As J.B. Schramm says, "It is so freeing when an organization has a culture where you can be direct. A culture where you can say what is on your mind with the full knowledge that no one will melt."

Here's some language you can use:

"I want to be truthful with you. This is how I feel on the topic of _____."

That's it. The truth is usually best told simply.

3. Set expectations and keep coming back to them.

You have the power to set expectations, and if you do, people will respond. It doesn't need to feel like you're herding rhinos; people won't die if they disagree with you, and if they do disagree, it can open up a positive dialogue. When you set expectations and reinforce them frequently, everybody wins.

Here's some language you can use:

"I expect that you will accomplish _____ by the end of the month. Can I count on you to do that?"

4. Use direct and empathic language.

It's possible to say, "No, thank you" without destroying a relationship with a supporter, a staff person, or a board member. Always thank people for their suggestions, and if their recommendations aren't aligned with what you feel your organization has to do, note them and let them go.

Here's some language you can use:

"Thanks for your suggestion. Given our current focus, we won't be able to pursue this opportunity, but I'll get back to you if we change our direction."

As Judith Sills[7] said, "Wielded wisely, *no* is an instrument of integrity, and a shield against exploitation. It often takes courage to say. It is hard to receive. But setting limits sets us free."

People who work in the nonprofit sector often feel that some unspoken obligation—or *quid pro quo*—is ready to surface. The result of this unspecified fear stunts power, muddles decision-making, and makes focus and clear communication difficult to harness.

Because they are often subtle and hard to pinpoint, the four beliefs and behaviors we've explored in this chapter can be damaging to an organization's ability to thrive. However, now armed with the tools to spot these challenges in yourself and in your colleagues,

---

[7] "The Power of No." *Psychology Today*, November 2013.

you'll be able to keep them in mind—and counterbalance them as they surface. Doing so will prepare you to chart a new vision for your organization's decision-making.

PUTTING IT ALL TOGETHER

Now that you've looked at the roots of your views on power and decision-making, and you've examined more deeply how your organization operates, you should have a fairly sound blueprint for where you are.

The challenge you face now is to create a vision for where you'd *like* to be.

As a leader in your organization, your job is to foster an environment where power and decision-making are clear. This is vital because, as you've seen with the four models explored in this chapter, it's impossible to optimize your effectiveness if these elements in your organization are disorganized and colored with resentment.

Having clarified these critical areas in your organization by completing the activities in this chapter, you're now ready to move on to understanding the decision-making ecosystem of your nonprofit.

KEY TAKEAWAYS

Like an iceberg whose full scale is impossible to see from the surface, many organizations are similarly unclear about who has power and who makes decisions.

Those who lead nonprofits have personal and professional influences that affect their views on power and decision-making—many of which are often unconscious or unexplored, and can have a weighty effect on a leader's perspective.

Four models of dysfunctional power and decision-making—each with its own costs and benefits—are common in nonprofits:

- My Way or the Highway
- Don't Make Me Come in There
- We're All in This Together
- You Can Do It

Most people in nonprofits are aware of how the structure of their organization functions, but they have no idea how to (or whether they can) talk about it publicly or change it for the better.

The need to demonstrate to supporters a sense of disproportional kindness, gratitude, and deference creates a sense of dependence that skews nonprofit decision-making.

Nonprofits can improve their decision-making by:

- Calmly bringing up uncomfortable topics
- Telling the truth, at all times
- Setting and staying focused on performance expectations
- Using direct and empathic language in dealing with all supporters

YOUR DECISION-MAKING
ECOSYSTEM

If you're a leader in your organization, this chapter is an opportunity for you to understand how power and decision-making currently work in your environment. Few people take the time to understand these elements in their organization from a systemic perspective, but if you take a proactive approach to understanding how your ecosystem actually operates, you'll get a clearer picture of what your options are, as well as the kinds of shifts you may want to make. If you don't currently have a leadership role, this chapter will enable you to visualize how your organization operates and your role in it.

In nature, an ecosystem is a complex set of relationships in an area that includes plants, trees, animals, fish, birds, micro-organisms, water, soil, and sometimes people. Ecosystems vary in their elements, but each is dependent on the others to create a functioning unit. In this way, your organization has a power and decision-making ecosystem made up of everyone who works in your organization and interacts with it. Different incentives motivate each member of your ecosystem, and each member exerts its influence in different ways.

Taking the time to understand your ecosystem and how it operates is an essential step in painting a clear picture of a different future. It can also give you perspective on whether you are utilizing the smart people you have in the best ways possible. While the executive director, board, leadership team, staff, volunteers, clients, and donors are all part of a system that shifts and flows depending on the issue at hand, it also shifts according to who is perceived as having power at any particular time.

DIAGRAMMING POWER

When people are given the task of diagramming the power structure of their nonprofit, they typically create something that looks like one of these:

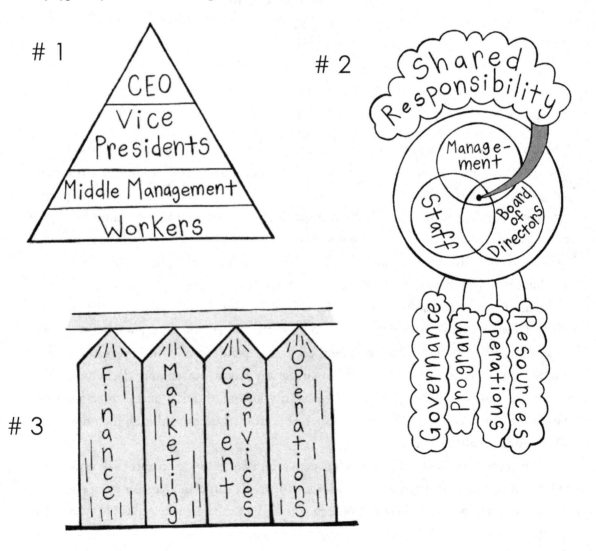

The problem with these diagrams is that they assume the viewer knows where power lives in the diagram, when it actually isn't called out. Being specific about where power resides in your organization is the first step in building a high-level picture of your ecosystem.

Chances are, you already have your own idea of how your power structure looks, and it may be similar to or different from the illustrations on the previous page. In the space provided below, draw your organization and highlight where power is situated in your particular ecosystem.

As you consider the structure, think about which people are most productive in your environment, which people others fear, who others go to for advice and counsel, and who gets asked to weigh in on important topics. Be honest and feel free to draw whatever you believe is true, without regard to what "traditional" diagrams look like.

Now, take a moment to reflect on each aspect of your diagram and on who in your organization has power, and who doesn't.

❖ Is there anything interesting or surprising that creating this visual model has brought to the surface?

❖ What is obvious about your organization's power and decision-making ecosystem from your drawing?

The Rules of Your Decision-Making Ecosystem

Every decision-making ecosystem has its spoken and unspoken rules. For example:

"If we don't make decisions together, we don't make them."

"The executive director makes all the decisions."

"We don't make a decision until we all agree."

"I'm not going to agree that we've made a decision until I get my way."

"I don't ever want my decisions to alienate anyone."

"How decisions get made in our organization varies day to day."

Think about your own ecosystem, and answer the following questions:

❖   What are the rules of your organization?

❖   How are these rules consciously or unconsciously reinforced?

❖   What happens to people who violate these rules?

❖ How do your current rules positively or negatively affect your organization?

Who Is in Your Decision-Making Ecosystem?

Now let's go a little deeper, and explore the actual decision-making participants in your organization. Here's a hint: every discrete group in your organization is part of your ecosystem, and each of these groups and the individuals contained within them may have a different perspective on which decisions they would like to make. A typical nonprofit decision-making ecosystem looks something like this:

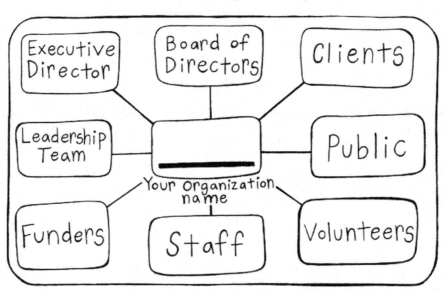

Decision-Making Ecosystem

- Executive Director
- Board of Directors
- Clients
- Leadership Team
- Your Organization name
- Public
- Funders
- Staff
- Volunteers

Now list some of the names of people in your ecosystem. We've provided title categories to get the ball rolling.

THE EXECUTIVE DIRECTOR

INDIVIDUAL BOARD MEMBERS

INDIVIDUAL LEADERSHIP TEAM MEMBERS

INDIVIDUAL STAFF MEMBERS

INDIVIDUAL VOLUNTEERS

INDIVIDUAL CLIENTS

INDIVIDUAL FUNDERS

If we break down your ecosystem in this way, even the smallest nonprofit has dozens of discrete decision-making members, making numerous big and small decisions every day of the week.

Who Makes the Decisions?

In the space provided below, consider the people in your ecosystem and the way power is distributed. Take a moment to reflect on the individuals you listed on the previous pages, and then draw another diagram of your organization's ecosystem that includes the people you've listed. This drawing could look a lot like the one you did earlier in this chapter (with more detail), or it could be a completely different drawing.

Now consider the following questions:

1. Who makes the important decisions in your organization?

2. Who has little, if any, decision-making authority?

3. Who has a big title, but makes very few decisions?

4. Who doesn't have a big title, and seems to make a lot of decisions?

5. Are the answers to any of these questions murky?

6. If the answers aren't clear, how much time do you waste trying to figure out who can make what decisions?

A Closer Look at the Elements

As we look deeper into the way your ecosystem actually works, you will notice that every element—the executive director, the board, the leadership team, the staff, the volunteers (if you have them), the clients, and the funders—each has particular needs, ways of operating, and decisions they would like to make. So let's start at the top.

The Executive Director

Whether the person at the helm of your organization is called an executive director or a CEO, there is someone who has the responsibility to lead the staff and interact with the board.

In most nonprofits, the executive director is the linchpin of the organization, the person who can create order from chaos and make things happen. Each executive director does things differently, but what all of them have in common is that they are trying to do too much. Many suffer from a lack of focus, and they react to a desire to do the right thing by either micromanaging or seeking consensus. While some have certainly implemented systems that are efficient, the truth is that few executive directors have a conscious plan for driving power and decision-making to the people who are closest to the decisions in the queue.

As you think about your executive director (or reflect on yourself if you have that role), consider the following questions:

❖ What are the important decisions this person has made in the last year?

❖ Does this person demonstrate decision-making focus or is s/he involved in decisions that should be decided by others?

❖ Has s/he encouraged other people to take responsibility for making decisions?

❖ How aligned are the board and the executive director in terms of their power and decision-making responsibilities? Is there conflict here?

The Board

Although there is no shortage of websites to help nonprofit boards perform efficiently (and many highly recommended books have been published on the subject), most nonprofit boards do *not* behave in a textbook fashion. Each board has specific features and behaviors, and their relationships with their executive directors are distinct.

While there are often great people serving on boards, we've observed that many operate inconsistently, sometimes with little clarity on which decisions they will make and which will be reserved for the executive director. Some boards micromanage and others under-manage, while still others are unsure of their decision-making responsibilities.

This confusion often stems from how individual board members view their service. Some believe that the executive director is the person who is responsible for driving the organization, and therefore should make almost all of the important decisions. While these boards understand their fiduciary responsibilities, they let the executive director set the agenda. These members believe their primary decision-making role is to hire or fire the executive director, sign off on the budget, and possibly raise money.

As a consequence, they show up and move down the quarterly agenda without complaint. Board decision-making is confined to the topics the executive director asks the board to weigh in on, and board members themselves assume they are there to support the executive director and to listen to (and mostly approve) his or her direction.

In other boards, members see themselves as representatives of the community who should be involved in every issue. This often occurs in boards that have members with strong personalities, as well as in organizations where there has been a revolving door of executive directors.

Within the spectrum of "weak" to "strong" boards, almost all fail to consistently and clearly demarcate which decisions are within the purview of the executive director and which belong to the board. This confusion is heightened by the service mentality of being on a nonprofit board. Since the members are "giving" to the organization, they may not hold themselves (or be held) to a stringent standard. Board meetings are often missed; monies fail to be donated, and yet boards stumble on. Rarely are members held accountable or asked to step down.

In their hearts, many nonprofit board members believe they are doing their organizations a "favor" through their service, and the organizations they serve implicitly agree. The prevailing wisdom is that most nonprofit board seats are difficult to fill, so organizations will take what participation and service they can get.

Moreover, unlike service on for-profit boards (where there's a prospect that board members will reap significant financial benefit from their participation, and where service rules are clearly enunciated and rigorously upheld), nonprofit board service makes no such promise. As a result, decision-making responsibilities of the board and the executive director are often confused. In light of these governance issues, consider the following questions:

❖ Have you seen the aforementioned dynamics at work in your organization?

❖ Take a moment to reflect on the past year. Which important decisions did your board make?

❖ Which decisions did your board avoid?

❖ Did anyone bring the board's decision-making challenges to their attention or did the leadership let it slide?

Now, if you're the executive director, it's critical that you put your attention on your board's chairperson. Every book written on board governance will tell you that developing and maintaining a strong relationship with your board chair is essential, and we agree—this is the person with whom you must get specific as to the division of your decision-making responsibilities. Thinking of your relationship with your board chair, consider the following questions:

❖ What decisions does your board chair make now?

❖ What decisions is s/he avoiding?

❖ If your board has committees, what decisions are within their responsibility? Are they clear which decisions they can make?

Now let's examine the individuals on your board. Individual members may have a particular interest in one or more initiatives, so you'll need to consider the following:

❖ Do you know what each member on your board is interested in and what decisions s/he would like to weigh in on? List them on the next page.

❖ How involved have your board members been in the important decisions facing your organization in the last year?

❖ How would you rate the quality of board member participation over the last year?

1	2	3	4	5
poor	fair	good	very good	excellent

Taking the time to answer these questions will give you a deeper perspective on how your board, its committees, and its individual members operate around decision-making. You will apply this insight in Part II.

The Leadership Team

Unless you're a small nonprofit, you likely have a team of senior managers who assist with the operations of your organization. Each of these individuals manages a critical aspect of your effort. While they may come together for weekly or monthly staff meetings, they most likely don't make decisions within the team context.

Members of the leadership team, on the other hand, are often asked for their opinions in a group setting. Unless they're empowered to vote, however, leadership teams don't often make decisions; rather, they tend to give advice in the staff-meeting setting, and their advice is accepted or rejected by the executive director. Sometimes the executive director allows the leadership team to think they have individually or collectively made a decision, when in truth s/he was making the decision and simply taking advice.

While the decision-making authority of a leadership team is often uncertain, each person does make decisions on behalf of the functions they supervise. Consider the following questions:

❖   If you look at the individual members of the leadership team, what important decisions has each person made in the last year?

❖   Do people at this level of your organization actually make decisions, or are they "implementers" who follow orders?

❖   Are the individual members of your leadership team fully aware of all the decisions they have to make?

❖ Do they feel empowered to make decisions, or are they constantly looking over their shoulders?

Be sure to reflect on your leadership team and the way they make decisions, individually and collectively.

The Staff

Staff plays a critical role in all nonprofits. If you think about the crucial decisions the members of your staff have made this past year, which ones come to mind? In the space provided, write down as much as you can about the decisions your staff makes by answering the following questions:

❖ What have been the important decisions made by individual staff members in the last year?

❖ Where has the staff encountered decision-making frustration?

❖ Is the staff being fully utilized in your decision-making process?

The Volunteers

Non-board member volunteer service is highly variable. Some nonprofits engage volunteers sporadically, and others are completely dependent on them. If your organization makes scant use of non-board volunteers, you can skip this section as it won't particularly apply to you.

If your organization makes extensive use of volunteers to run your programs or to raise money (or any of the myriad tasks that volunteers manage), be aware that you and your organization have either consciously or unconsciously vested power and decision-making authority in them.

Nonprofit volunteers can be quite assertive in their pursuit of your mission. If you haven't been clear about what decisions these volunteers are allowed to make, rest assured that they are likely exercising power and making decisions on your organization's behalf. Consider the following questions:

❖ What decisions do your individual volunteers currently make?

❖ Are you happy with the decisions they are making?

❖ What are the decisions you would like your volunteer community to make?

The Clients

Like the use of volunteers, the power and decision-making responsibilities of nonprofit clients can vary tremendously. Whether your client is a school district, a section of the community, or an individual, these entities rightly seek to influence how your services are delivered—and their influence can be enormous. Some nonprofits utilize client councils to help shape their offerings; others have ad hoc contact with the people they serve and rarely create opportunities for clients to participate in decision-making. Consider the following questions and write down your answers:

❖ Are you conscious of how much your clients influence your decision-making, and how much you take them into account?

❖ Does your nonprofit offer any decision-making opportunities to your clients? If so, which decisions and to whom?

❖ Do you want your clients to serve in an advisory or decision-making role?

The Funders

Yes, your funders also have a role in your organization's decision-making. Often nonprofits solicit desperately needed foundation or other donor dollars, even if these funds come with strings attached. True, donors can't affect your decision-making environment if you don't take their money, but many nonprofits do, and then try to deal as best they can with the restrictions that come along with these donations.

Unlike the other members of your decision-making ecosystem, funders can only influence your decision-making environment to the extent that you let them into your organization. For many this isn't a choice. If yours does accept funds that have restrictions, you are bound to be influenced by these funders.

Consider the following questions and jot down your thoughts:

❖ How have your funders influenced your organization's operational focus and decision-making?

❖ What have been the benefits and costs of this influence?

YOUR ORGANIZATION'S DECISION-MAKING ECOSYSTEM

Now that you have a detailed overview of how your organization makes decisions, fill out the blank ecosystem chart below. Then, take a step back and look at the big picture of your ecosystem, as well as the details.

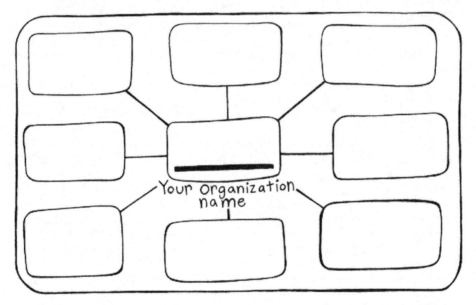

❖ Are you happy with how decisions are divided in your ecosystem?

❖ If you could change the decision pattern of the groups or individuals in your ecosystem, would you do so?

If your answer to that last question is yes, you have identified an opportunity for growth, and Decision Clarity can help you get there.

Next, look at your ecosystem and consider who is allowed to make decisions and who isn't.

❖ Are there groups or individuals who are NOT permitted to make important decisions?

❖ If yes, make a list of the people or departments that are excluded from making important decisions.

o Why are they in this category?

    o   Do you want to add to or subtract from their ability to make decisions in your organization's ecosystem?

Now consider these pointed questions:

❖ Do all the elements of your ecosystem know which decisions they can make?

❖ Have your leaders been clear about how they want to divide decision-making within the overall ecosystem?

For many people, a detailed look at their power and decision-making ecosystem can be a sobering experience. Many leaders are uneasy about altering the current framework because of the perceived fragility of their organization, but there's no need to fear these changes. Decision Clarity will serve as your guide to walk you through the steps to alter decision-making in your ecosystem in a way that will preserve the positive elements of your organization's ways of operating, while allowing you to capitalize on the energy that may still be locked up in the current structure of your ecosystem.

As you seek to improve the structure of your organization, you are certain to encounter some resistance to change. In the following chapter we will look at some of the obstacles you may face—and how to manage them—arming you with ways to make the transition positive for everyone.

KEY TAKEAWAYS

Decision-making ecosystems have specific operational rules that aren't written down yet are crucial to understand.

Decision-making ecosystems continue to evolve as new people enter and exit the organization and new priorities emerge.

All nonprofits have a distinct power and decision-making ecosystem that determines how decisions are made.

People come to understand the "rules" of their ecosystem by observing who has power and who makes decisions in their organizations.

Even when nonprofit leaders try to obfuscate the power and decision-making rules of their organization, their team members readily pick up on what is happening.

Mapping out this ecosystem in detail and answering straightforward questions about who is currently included and excluded in your organization's decision-making process is a great way to get clarity and find hidden dynamics that can remain invisible.

It's important to pinpoint who is in your decision-making ecosystem and know what decisions they want to make or support. This includes the board, leadership team, staff, volunteers, clients, and funders.

Diagramming your own eco-system will give you a better sense of what you know, what you don't know, and where you may want to focus.

4

DEALING WITH CONFLICT

Imagine this: You're driving on a familiar road and talking away on your phone about a situation at work. At some point, you recognize you're getting to a spot where the reception always breaks off. You say to your colleague on the other end, "Hey, I'm getting close to where my calls always drop." You and your coworker either wrap up the call, or agree to call back once you get past the difficult area.

Sound familiar? Of course it does. We often do this without even thinking twice about the matter-of-fact steps we take to resolve these types of situations. So let's take a moment to examine what actually happens in a dropped-call scenario.

- ❖ First, we use our "institutional" knowledge of the road and our phone coverage to be mindful of where our calls have previously dropped.

- ❖ Second, we calmly communicate this development to the person on the other end of the line. Even if we're talking about something of great urgency, we aren't flustered by the need to at least temporarily conclude the call. We aren't confused about what we should do; we see a challenge and take care of it.

- ❖ Third, we make a rational plan that serves the needs of both parties. We offer to end the call before the service drops or to reconnect later. We suggest a solution and smoothly move through the interaction without hesitation, fear, or confusion. In a matter of seconds, we anticipate the problem, communicate our concern to the other party, and advocate a rational plan to resolve this challenge of everyday life.

As you can see, this isn't a complicated process; you've used this method many times for dropped calls and countless other issues and obstacles you face every day. What's interesting is that when you get to these small roadblocks in life, you don't become unglued. There's not a lot of drama, confusion, or fear. You don't worry about whether you have the power to say something concerning what you already know, or whether you can make a decision. You use your knowledge to communicate with the person you're engaged with, and create a plan that will serve both your needs.

So if this strategy works, why can't we use it when facing other potentially more intense challenges? Is there any reason why we can't employ the same method to identify where power and decision-making conflict and confusion lurk in your organization?

Of course, power conflicts at work are typically more challenging and emotionally laden than a dropped phone call. There may be a great deal at stake, and you might not be able to predict how the conflict could be resolved. But in the same way you can't always predict when a call will drop, or when a power and decision-making tussle may ensue, you already know a great deal about where the power "dead spots" are in your organization, and that even if you ignore them, they will continue to exist.

In this chapter, we'll talk about how you can use your *institutional knowledge* to predict your most troubling areas of power and decision-making conflict and confusion. We'll do this so you can start preparing to *communicate* about them, and to develop a *rational plan* to deal with them. If you've recently joined your organization and feel like you're still learning about your ecosystem, ask the members of your team where the conflicts and confusion in your organization exist. You'll find that it's not a mystery—all you have to do is ask.

Let's be frank—after completing the activities in the previous chapter, you already have a sense of where you're going to run into power and decision-making issues in your organization. And if you dwell on it, you're likely to feel some anxiety, instead of reacting to it as if it were a simple dropped call. We don't believe it needs to be this way. If you can anticipate where conflict and confusion lurk, you are one step closer to addressing these concerns carefully and thoughtfully.

CONFLICTS ARE COMMON

Disputes pop up all the time; they'll never be avoided completely. So while we wouldn't suggest you can eliminate conflict, our goal is to help you become more aware of where conflict already exists in your organization. Once you do, you can become more conscious of these issues and be prepared to address them later when we walk through the Decision Clarity process. We also want to help you become more aware of your unconscious reactions to conflict so that you can keep them in mind as you make choices and move forward.

To set the stage, let's look at how you tend to react when faced with power and decision-making conflicts.

YOUR REACTION TO POWER AND DECISION-MAKING CONFLICTS

In Chapter 2, you learned how your views on power and decision-making drive how your organization thinks about these topics; the people around you also note how you act in response to power and decision-making uncertainty. People listen to what you say, but they pay even more attention to how you act.

Sometimes, the conflict is explicit (I want to do X and you want me to do Y), and other times, the conflicts are born out of confusion (I'd like to decide on X and I have no idea if I have the authority to do it). Sometimes, people simply don't agree on who has the power to make a decision (I want to decide X and you want to decide X). These are just a few examples of the conflicts and confusion that can exist.

Aside from the four models of dysfunctional decision-making culture we outlined in Chapter 2, there are four prominent leadership decision-making styles that relate to these cultures. When conflict or confusion boils up in organizations around decision-making, our experience has taught us that executive directors and nonprofit leaders typically gravitate to one of four principal styles—or frames.

The style adopted by a nonprofit leader is often influenced by the extent to which this person fears failure, conflict, or rejection. If there is staff resistance, we have found that leaders can indeed switch out of their primary role and take on another, but people generally start in their comfort zone, and, if necessary, adapt from there.

The four styles/frames follow.

Style 1:

Autocrat

Nonprofit leaders in this frame believe that they alone should make all the important decisions, and they reserve the right to involve themselves anywhere at any time. Executive directors in this frame want to be the repository of power in *all* decision-making issues. Why? Because they don't believe they can take the time to establish responsibilities for themselves *and* for others—it's "simpler" for them to merely make the decision.

When a nonprofit leader is in the Autocrat frame, board and staff members who are aware of their leader's style will only take on decisions that they know *for a fact* they are cleared to make. They likewise know that if there is any decision-making conflict, their leader will jump in and resolve it. At the first sign of trouble, they will pause and simply wait for their leader to settle the matter.

In the Autocrat frame, staff and board initiative goes largely untapped. Ecosystem members become so used to indiscriminate intervention that they typically wait to see what the leader is going to do. Sometimes, leaders who take this stance don't want to be seen in this autocratic light, so instead of jumping in, they will "guide" their staff to decisions that they favor—giving the illusion of collaboration and consensus, when in fact, they are forcing a particular outcome.

Style 2:

Nonprofit leaders in this frame would rather appease those who jockey for power and decision-making than lay out a replicable framework for apportioning these powers in their environment. Occupants of this frame are easily swayed by the people in their organization making the most noise, or rather, the ones who are opinionated and are willing to engage in conflict to gain an advantage.

Leaders who are Appeasers respond to their power and decision-making conflicts in an uncoordinated fashion. Since they don't have a strategy, they merely move from one crisis to another. Occupants of this frame are not only uncomfortable with organizational confrontation, but they also have great difficulty with conflict on a personal level.

Appeasers tend to value consensus and concepts of shared decision-making—often seeking solutions that will offend the fewest people, but tending to avoid decisions that could be controversial yet have a more positive impact on the organization.

Style 3:

Nonprofit leaders in this frame like to postpone potential conflicts, or avoid them all together. They understand where the flash points are in their ecosystem, but they prefer not to deal with these issues. Occupants of this frame are often uncomfortable with confrontation, or they think their organization is too fragile to engage successfully on the topic. It's easy to delay uncomfortable power and decision-making challenges in the hopes that the delay will allow things to "work themselves out" over time.

Board members and staff who are aware that their executive director is an Avoider know that any decision-making process that they or the organization engages in will be long and circuitous. Typically, Avoider executive directors seek to eliminate controversy by promoting a consensus-based decision. Board and staff will typically take the lead on non-controversial decisions, but they know that decisions that ruffle feathers will need to be exhaustively and carefully vetted.

As with the Autocrat style, staff and board initiative go largely untapped. Ecosystem members become so used to avoidance techniques that they wait to see whether the leader is actually serious about making a decision. This style can create staff exhaustion, especially when there is conflict. Here, the staff learns to avoid making difficult decisions because the leader is avoiding them. Moreover, the headache of driving to a difficult conclusion when faced with the leader's uncertainty is seen as requiring too much effort for too small a payoff to be worth undertaking.

Style 4:

Micro-Manager

Nonprofit leaders in this frame believe that there is no decision too small for them to be involved in. Micromanagers will insert themselves into any number of issues because they fear failure and desire a high level of control. In contrast to Autocrats, who believe all power emanates from them, the Micromanagers will jump in inconsistently.

When a leader is a Micromanager, many senior staff members feel that s/he will meddle in their affairs and not trust them to make decisions or to implement them correctly. Staff assumes that the executive director will, at any moment, step in to overturn or modify their decisions. In conflict situations, staff members know that they may have to defend their position against the sometimes irrational desire on the part of the leader to control everything.

In the Micromanager frame, staff and board initiative are inconsistently used. Some controversial issues get over-direction, and some issues are ignored. There are no clear signposts that inform the other participants when Micromanagers will roll up their sleeves and muck around in the decision-making process. They frequently get spooked and will act on their fear and biases suddenly and vigorously.

Consider the following questions and write your answers in the space provided:

❖ If you're an executive director or member of the leadership team, do you find yourself in one or more of these typologies?

❖ If you're an executive director or member of the leadership team, where do you find yourself most comfortable?

  o What have been the costs and benefits to you and your organization of adopting this approach?

If you're a board member or a staff person:

❖ Does your executive director inhabit one of these styles? Which one(s)?

❖ What have been the costs and benefits to you and the organization of the executive director (or your manager) adopting this approach?

❖ If your executive director (or manager) occupies one of these styles, how would you like their decision-making behavior to change?

AREAS OF POWER AND DECISION-MAKING CONFLICT

In 2004, Thomas Barnett authored his landmark work, *The Pentagon's New Map.* In it he proposed a framework for how the United States could operate to reduce violence and increase international cooperation. One of Barnett's key findings was that "violence decreases as rules are established for dealing with international conflicts." It may be obvious, but creating a structure and rules that will guide behavior creates better outcomes.

While the focus of this highly acclaimed work is centered on nations, the ideas can also apply to nonprofit organizations.

The purpose of the rest of this chapter is to call out some of the more prominent areas of conflict and confusion so that if they are present in your nonprofit, you can make note of them when using the Decision Clarity process.

The common areas where conflict and confusion can lurk are:

❖ Diversity and Privilege

❖ Executive Director and Board Relations

❖ Executive Director and Leadership Relations

❖ Leadership and Staff Relations

❖ Local and Regional Office Relations

❖ Organization and Volunteer Relations

Not all of these conflict points will exist in your ecosystem at the same time, and some may not exist at all. But these are typical areas of conflict in nonprofits, and they are worth keeping in mind, especially those that are most relevant to you.

Diversity and Privilege

Most nonprofit organizations serve those who are at a disadvantage in our society. Traditional nonprofits fill societal gaps that government and business can't or won't address. As such, nonprofits naturally have a strong interest in equalizing opportunity, and raising up those who have fewer advantages in our society. Many of the staff of these nonprofits come from these "disadvantaged" or "diverse" communities.

In our societal shorthand, we contrast "diverse communities" with "communities of privilege." Those in a community of privilege enjoy longstanding advantages in our society that aren't necessarily questioned. These privileges become part of how we live, work, love—and how we think about power and make decisions. These privileges focus on areas of gender (male), race (white), class (middle or upper), age (middle), education (higher), able-bodied (not disabled), or sexual/gender orientation (straight). While there are many forms of privilege other than the ones we've just mentioned, these tend to be recognized as the major differentiating characteristics—and the people with these privileges usually make most of the decisions.

What this means in terms of conflict and confusion around power and decision-making is profound. Nonprofit employees often represent the constituencies served by their organization. But while these entry- or mid-level employee populations are diverse, the senior positions are often filled with people of privilege. Given the concentrated nature of nonprofit power and decision-making in most organizations, this means the people who are *making* a majority of the decisions for their organization tend to be those with more privilege and societal advantage, while those *carrying out* the decisions tend to be those from more diverse backgrounds.

Not surprisingly, the mention of "privilege" provokes some degree of strife, fear, and discomfort in nonprofits whose leadership is predominantly represented by people with race, class, age, education, and sexual orientation benefits. This is particularly true for white employees from privileged backgrounds who want to appear to be above reproach, or nonprofit leaders who, when asked about the lack of diversity on the board or senior leadership, respond with some version of, "Why are you grinding me on issues like diversity when I'm trying to change the world?"

The topic of privilege in your organization can not only bring up a lot of feelings, but also collective guilt for the historical mistreatment of people from diverse backgrounds. It can also throw a harsh light on the fact that your organization may not be making as much progress as it would like to in becoming more diverse. More subtly, the topic of diversity can surface long-held negative stereotypes and beliefs about the capacities of those from diverse populations. It can also bring up fear that the diverse members may harbor fundamentally different viewpoints or disrupt the status-quo.

At its core, the topic of privilege can be seen as code for "power shift" and this is threatening to even the most well-intentioned people. If you have power, the typical first imperative is to keep it. This is particularly true if you don't have a way to talk about and redistribute power in a comfortable way. And while many people don't have a philosophical problem with creating greater diversity in their organizations, they often don't know how to do it without affecting the existing power structures.

Employees at the bottom of the organizational hierarchy are rarely offered the opportunity to make important or even grade-level decisions. In fact, we often hear that people feel they need to leave their nonprofit to be promoted to a level of more responsibility. And because diversity and privilege tend to have a bigger impact on decision-making than even executive director and board relations, it's considered a top priority when examining conflict in an organization.

Executive Director and Board Relations

Conflict and confusion frequently exist between boards and executive directors, but unless the organization is failing or the executive director needs to be replaced, they tend to merely fester beneath the surface.

Few board members bring these unresolved points of contention into the open unless they have to. It's common to find boards and executive directors in a position of indirectly "feeling each other out" to understand the limits of their power and their ability to make decisions. They may not know where the lines are so they move from issue to issue, reinventing these boundaries as they go.

As David Styers, formerly a senior board governance consultant for the Center for Volunteer and Nonprofit Leadership and now with The Presidio Institute, says, "Most nonprofit boards want to put their heads in the sand unless there is a pressing problem. And most executive directors would rather be unchallenged, and have their boards look at their work through rose-colored glasses."

Hence, while the board may know that it has to approve the organization's budget, provide an executive director evaluation, raise money, and maintain general oversight, there is rarely consistency in board operations, and decision-making isn't often discussed in clear language, nor in a forthright and productive way.

As an example, one of our clients had a board that was dedicated to the organization's mission, but saw their primary function to support the initiatives of the executive director. As they were always waiting for instructions instead of taking initiative, they would merely do what was asked of them without pushing the executive director or themselves to raise money or develop new programs. As a result, term limits were not enforced, feedback was inconsistently offered, and fundraising goals were seldom met.

The executive director felt it was impolite to bring up these shortcomings, and the board, in turn, was exhausted from both long service and confused priorities. With no set expectations, it was easier just to be told what to do. And while this board was populated with senior, successful, for-profit people, they nonetheless tolerated a level of power and decision-making confusion that they would never accept in their for-profit endeavors.

> This is just one example of where executive director/board conflict and confusion can hide; it also points to the human dynamics that keep these tensions going. We've seen executive director/board conflict pop up in a variety of ways, but the most common areas are conflicts over mission, program implementation, metrics, and executive director feedback.

Executive Director and Leadership Relations

Many executive directors and their leadership teams experience significant conflict and confusion at times, but the issues are often muted by the commitment to their shared mission. In trying to project a unified vision and operational perspective to the members of their ecosystem, they tend to stick together. While a premium is placed on this level of cohesion, this stance often masks conflict and confusion over decisions.

We've seen a variety of unhelpful dynamics between executive directors and their leadership teams—including executive directors who use their leadership meetings as venting sessions, but never ask individual leaders to make a decision, as well as those who mask their commitment to a particular decision by inviting collaboration, yet trusting that their own perspective will prevail.

In contrast, we've also witnessed leadership teams who discuss issues until they are completely exhausted, rarely making a decision that isn't revisited later. We've also seen individual team members who are given explicit authority to make decisions, but will often wait to gain approval of the executive director, thus stalling the process. The combinations are endless, but the themes are often the same—conflict, confusion, and usually some evidence of fear of failure.

Leadership and Staff Relations

Individual leadership team members and their staff also make conscious and un-conscious agreements about how power and decision-making will function in their group. Each team has a different level of tolerance around confusion, and each tackles conflict in varying ways.

Some leaders effectively delegate power and decision-making to the members of their team, while others reserve the right to make all the important decisions with their team members being implementers of their vision. In this way, the dynamics with the executive director can be mirrored in the leadership/staff relations. As a result, staff who would normally have a reasonable expectation to take on power and decision-making within their unit become hesitant to advocate for it, not to mention that fear of failure can actually drive decision-making up the management chain.

Sometimes, unspoken elements of power can be the stumbling block. For example, in one leadership team we worked with, an experienced and respected staff member had great difficulty advocating for decision-making authority that should have been hers. This supervisor oversaw a team of approximately 20 employees, and nearly all important decisions that affected her team should have been within her purview. But even though the executive director urged the supervisor to advocate for more authority, this person resisted.

When questioned, the supervisor said it wasn't because she didn't want the extra work; she simply "didn't want to be seen as grasping for power." For this person (in this ecosystem), it was uncomfortable to be perceived as an advocate for decision-making, although she was encouraged to do so and it would benefit the mission and her clients. After giving voice to this concern and discussing it with the leadership team, she was able to confidently advocate for herself and began to make the important decisions that affected the quality of programs in her organization.

> Leadership/staff conflicts typically pop up in program strategy and implementation, program metrics, scheduling, or marketing and branding.

Regional and National Office and Staff Relations

As nonprofit organizations grow, they often develop a regional office function. This happens most frequently in high-performing, rapidly expanding nonprofits. Clients and funders see results and encourage expansion, but rarely does this happen with explicit dividing lines for which office has specific decision-making power, and who can make which decisions.

Sometimes this confusion is simply the result of expansion that happens quickly, when no one has taken the time to spell out how decision-making needs to work. Other times, regional offices are staffed with local people who feel a passionate need to solve a community or regional problem; as such, these individuals want to bring the full measure of their commitment and creativity to their work. Regional office staff can quickly come to view national staff as "overhead" and an unnecessary enforcing authority. From the perspective of regional teams, the real action is at the local level, and they know what's best.

National office staff, in turn, can be frustrated when regional offices begin to presume power and decision-making responsibilities that are in conflict with their direction or approach. National offices presume they have these powers unless they explicitly give them away.

Confusion inherent in these topics can last for years as regional functions buckle under the direction of a strong national office. As an example, we once spoke with a rapidly expanding, metrics-driven, highly successful charter school organization. This nonprofit was facing an ongoing power and decision-making struggle between their school principals and national office. Even though they had grown successfully and had engaged on the topic on a number of occasions, they had been unable to reach an appropriate resolution. The CEO of the organization knew that he could enforce his will, but he hesitated to do so for fear of alienating one function over the other. In short, this highly successful organization was wasting valuable time and effort by their inability to resolve this issue.

> Typically, the tension between regional and national management shows up in decisions around budget, how much regional fundraising has to go to support national infrastructure, who the spokesperson is for a particular program, and how programs get implemented at the regional level.

Organization and Volunteer Relations

Nonprofits rely on members of their community to serve as volunteers. For some, the only volunteers they interact with are on their board, while others lean on volunteers for their service delivery, advocacy, and fundraising.

It's not unusual for volunteers to become fully invested in the way the organization delivers services, raises money, and operates programs, and when changes are necessary, they can raise significant resistance. Volunteers are often unclear about what power they have and which decisions need to be made by the organization. More importantly, some organizations are *intentionally* vague about this, for fear of alienating this vital part of the organization's ecosystem.

> In our experience, conflicts in organization/volunteer relations often lurk in program delivery, fundraising, volunteer involvement, and program expansion.

YOUR CONFLICT AND CONFUSION INVENTORY

Now that we've pointed out many of the hidden corners where conflict and confusion reside, you may notice that you had strong reactions to certain sections and mild reactions to others. Coupled with completion of the previous activities in the book, you likely now have a good sense of where the hot spots of conflict exist in your organization.

Where Conflict and Confusion Exist

The six main areas where conflict and confusion reside are within/between:

- Diversity and Privilege
- The Executive Director and Board
- The Executive Director and Leadership
- Leadership and Staff
- The Local and Regional Office
- The Organization and Its Volunteers

Given these areas, consider the following:

- Where are the major instances of power and decision-making conflict right now? Be as specific as you can, pinpointing particular decisions if you need to.

- Where is there confusion—both generally and personally? Make a note of how long this confusion has been in place.

On the forms below, take your observations and rank them on a scale of 1 to 5, with 1 reflecting no sense of conflict/confusion and 5 reflecting an extreme level.

Conflict Related to:

Gender, Race, Privilege

1_____2_____3_____4_____5

Executive Director and Board

1_____2_____3_____4_____5

Executive Director and Leadership

1_____2_____3_____4_____5

Leadership & Staff

1_____2_____3_____4_____5

Local and Regional Office

1_____2_____3_____4_____5

Organization and Volunteers

1_____2_____3_____4_____5

Confusion Related to:

Gender, Race, Privilege

1_____2_____3_____4_____5

Executive Director and Board

1_____2_____3_____4_____5

Executive Director and Leadership

1_____2_____3_____4_____5

Leadership & Staff

1_____2_____3_____4_____5

Local and Regional Office

1_____2_____3_____4_____5

Organization and Volunteers

1_____2_____3_____4_____5

Tally each form.

- ❖ What's your average score for the conflicts you listed?

- ❖ Which are the areas that have the highest degree of confusion?

- ❖ Ask a close colleague to review your forms. See if this person generally agrees with your assessment or would provide different ratings.

The absence of a clear path to resolve conflicts lets power and decision-making disputes and confusion simmer for years. Everyone knows where the "dead zones" are, but an aversion to conflict keeps people silent. Decision Clarity addresses this effectively, helping you know exactly *what* you need to talk about to prepare for these conversations.

Having fully assessed the components of power, decision-making, your ecosystem, and conflict with regard to your particular nonprofit, you are now ready to embark on transforming it into the efficient, harmonious, effective organization that will best serve your leadership, team, and those you are striving to help most—your beneficiaries.

KEY TAKEAWAYS

When you're more aware of where conflict already exists in your nonprofit, you can be conscious of these issues and prepared to address them later when you learn the Decision Clarity process.

When faced with conflict, leaders often react by falling into one or more of four unhelpful typologies:

- Autocrat
- Appeaser
- Avoider
- Micromanager

Decision-making conflicts can exist within every aspect of nonprofit operations, including:

- Diversity and Privilege
- Executive Director and Board
- Executive Director and Leadership Team
- Leadership and Staff
- Local and Regional/National Office
- Organization and Volunteers

It is also helpful to become more aware of your **unconscious** reactions to conflict, so that you can keep these in mind as you make choices and move forward.

PART TWO

Refocusing and Re-energizing

Your Organization

Using Decision Clarity

5

HOW DECISION CLARITY CAN TRANSFORM YOUR ORGANIZATION

As you've read and reflected on the chapters in Part I and answered questions about yourself and your nonprofit, you've no doubt pinpointed areas for opportunity. Rather than perceiving these as weaknesses in your organization, think of them as catalysts for making positive change. After all, if you're not aware of what *isn't* working, it's pretty difficult to discern what *is*. But now that you've uncovered where you'd like evolution to occur, you may be wondering, *What exactly is Decision Clarity and how can it transform our organization?*

In a nutshell, Decision Clarity is a new way of thinking—a process and a set of activities designed to clarify power and decision-making in nonprofits. What's more, it is not a practice that has been imported from the for-profit world and retrofitted for nonprofits; rather, it's a method that has been specifically crafted to harness the energy and passion of nonprofit employees and their boards.

When your organization applies and maintains the use of the Decision Clarity practice, you reap five major benefits:

❖ You better attract a diverse and talented staff, which strengthens every aspect of your nonprofit.

❖ You save both time and money in training and execution of tasks, big and small, because your decision-making structure is clear to everyone.

❖ You enjoy higher employee retention, reduced turnover, and stronger commitment to the cause.

❖ You cultivate a more diverse team of leaders from the bottom up, which benefits both the organization and the sector you serve.

❖ You discover faster and more effective decision-making and better collaboration among all team members.

So how did we arrive at this powerful method?

Decision Clarity was born out of a personal fascination with how decisions get made and who makes them. After years of working in nonprofits, this fascination matured into a dedicated mission to help leaders of nonprofits become more effective in what they do.

The catalyzing event, however, was in 2010, when my colleagues and I conducted a survey in collaboration with Commongood Careers (the nonprofit search firm) to assess the state of decision-making in nonprofits. A selection of quotes from the 218 respondents of that survey follow. Make a note as to whether you find these statements familiar or applicable to your own organization.

> "I left my last job (COO at a nonprofit) because there was a lack of clarity about my role and which decisions were mine. As COO, my decisions were often undermined by the CEO."

> "I constantly feel like I'm not empowered. I'm frustrated by it. I don't know how big decisions are made, and I'm not at the table making them."

> "I'm not allowed any opportunity to contribute to decisions even though I have valuable information and perspectives."

> "The lack of authority to make decisions makes my job significantly less satisfying, and it was a big factor in my decision to look for a job at another organization."

> "My organization is heavily into 'top-down' decision-making, and it's counter-productive to any sense of being a real team."

When we saw these comments, we set out to understand the complex issues underlying these findings—and to formulate a solution. What follows are the quantitative results from that survey. As you review them, consider what the leaders and staff in your own organization may report if you were to ask them these questions:

Are you sometimes confused about the decisions you can make?

If you look at the top 10 decisions that impact your job, do you generally make these decisions?

Does your confusion about the decisions you can make create inefficiency in your personal performance?

Does your confusion about the decisions you can make create operational inefficiency in your organization?

Has your organization tried to proactively identify the decisions you can make?

One of the interesting insights from this survey was the extent to which nonprofit members felt decision-making confusion made them less effective in their jobs. It further revealed that lack of certainty in the area of decision-making has a negative effect on how people feel about their jobs and their own individual performance.

Another finding was that employees tend to believe that their managers know more than they do, and they conclude that managers have clear paths to decision-making when our consulting work shows that this is actually *not true*. Middle and senior managers are often almost as much in the dark as their subordinates; as such, everyone in the organization can benefit from improved and clarified practices.

A third set of insights centers on the discovery that people are often not making decisions that go with their titles. As it turns out, just because you have a vice president, director, or manager title doesn't mean you're actually allowed to make the important decisions that affect your job and your team. This mismatch between roles and the decisions they are allowed to make represents a waste of talent and time—two resources vital to the health of every nonprofit.

As a solution to these issues, you will be introduced in the chapters to come to the specific skills of the Decision Clarity practice, with step-by-step instructions on how to easily implement it in your particular organization. Each chapter will build on the previous one, presenting the importance of each skill with activities that are fun, yet crucial to get you ready for the succeeding chapter. Your completion of the activities will culminate in the creation of a Decision Clarity grid, which will be your final map for implementing Decision Clarity in your organization.

As you begin the learning process, you may be tempted to charge ahead and skip certain portions, but we caution you against doing this. Like any new method, the component parts fit together in a particular way, and you need an understanding of each to apply every aspect of this work to your advantage. As you read each chapter and perform the activities, you will discover how the minimal investment of time you're making now will pay off manyfold in the future. The imbalance of power, conflict, and confusion around decision-making that is keeping you up at night and making your role less than optimal will be a thing of the past. Everyone will win.

Here is a high-level summary of what we will cover:

❖ Inventorying Decisions

❖ Prioritizing Decisions

❖ Self-Advocacy

❖ Creating a Decision Clarity Grid

❖ Engaging and Communicating with Your Team to Build a Unified Method of Decision-Making

By the end of Chapter 12, you will be equipped with all the tools you need to create an effective decision-making ecosystem—one where everyone understands what important decisions need to be made, and who has the power and authority to make them.

Sound good?

It gets even better!

One of the many perks about Decision Clarity is that it's a positive one for all involved. Each step invites an opportunity to discover what is actually happening in your organization, and to open up conversations around topics previously hidden from view.

The result? Surprise. Challenge. Liberation. Focus. Relief. And in the end, your whole team can perform at a higher level because people now have a shared language and a consistent method for thinking and communicating about power and decision-making.

What's more, we know that nonprofits spend countless hours arguing for, disputing, and wrestling with decision-making, so you will be thrilled to know it takes the average person no more than 15 *hours* to learn and implement the first four steps above. When you imagine the enormous amount of time wasted on inefficient practices that almost never produce beneficial results, 15 hours is a minimal investment for long-term clarity that will reinvigorate the focus of all who make up your beloved organization. Broken down into three-hour intervals, you could have this method up and running in your nonprofit in only one week's time. *One* week! Can you feel your stress level evaporating already?

As noted above, Decision Clarity requires that you and your team be able to **I**nventory, **P**rioritize, **A**dvocate for, and **C**ommunicate decisions that affect your jobs. We call these skills IPAC 4 Impact.

Here is a breakdown of what you can look forward to mastering:

Skill 1: Inventorying Decisions

When you perform an inventory, you list all the major decisions that affect your job and see the totality of what is on your plate.

In every nonprofit we've worked with, people are overwhelmed with the nature of their work, and it doesn't even occur to them to take inventory of all the issues they are attempting to decide, not to mention all the decisions that are buried within these issues. Once these decisions are on paper in front of you, you have taken the first step in creating order.

> Most everyone finds it illuminating to be able to make his or her list. Writing it all down somehow makes the whole process less frightening and more manageable.

Skill 2: Prioritizing Decisions

When you prioritize, you become clear on the high-impact decisions at hand. You then have the option to advocate for those decisions or entrust them to others. By prioritizing, you obtain a clear understanding of which decisions you need to make, and which you should remove from your current responsibility.

Not all decisions are important, and many nonprofits confuse action with progress when they focus on numerous small issues instead of a few major ones. Because vital decisions are often controversial and bring up the potential for conflict, people will frequently defer key decisions for protracted periods of time. Being able to openly consider which issues are the most important is essential for mobilizing your efforts to concentrate on the high-impact decisions that will move your organization forward.

> Prioritizing is often both challenging and liberating—challenging because nonprofits are often not encouraged to prioritize, because there's always more to be done; liberating because when people come to understand they can create order in their responsibilities, it's a freeing perspective.

Skill 3: Advocating for Decision-Making Roles and Responsibility

Advocating is a skill that requires you (and others) to ask for a specific role in a specific decision, and to provide an explanation for why you (or they) are best suited to perform that role. The language of advocating follows a prescribed structure, and while it helps streamline the process of decision making, it also provides a forum for your team to give voice to the decisions they want to make, and to secure feedback from their teammates about whether they can gain permission to assume this authority.

> People are astonished to find that advocating does not have to be a tension-filled process. When they use specific language, they can learn to advocate calmly and defend their assertions; they also learn that if they're not granted the decision-making responsibilities they want, the world won't cave in. They also enjoy expressing their views and speaking up to say that they now want to seek a role in decisions not previously afforded to them.

Creating Decision Clarity Grids

When you complete the activities within the first three skills, you'll be ready to complete a grid that is filled out with the key decisions facing you in your organization. The grid will document who on the team will make those decisions happen, and in what capacities they will serve.

Skill 4: Communicating for Clarity

Communicating your Decision Clarity grids is a simple two-step process. First, if you're the executive director, team leader, or manager, you will review the grids and confirm that the right people who are closest to a decision have appropriately advocated for it. (Grids can be changed in review if needed, but our experience shows that 90% of what people advocate for, they get approval for. So while grids can change, they don't change by much.)

The second step is to actually communicate. This means that the grids are shared and discussed as a group once they are final. This allows everyone on the team to know who has signed up for what decisions, which keeps the entire team in alignment. You will be provided a number of approaches for effectively communicating your grids in Chapter 11.

> For the first time, the team has a complete list of the decisions they have to tackle and who will play what role in their implementation. People usually find this knowledge a relief to have—and even more relieving that the knowledge is shared.

ASSUMING A ROLE IN THE D-E-C-I-D MODEL

By championing decisions you want to make (or support), regardless of your current position in the organization, you will fill one of five roles in the Decision Clarity D-E-C-I-D model.

Decision-maker   Expert/Advisor   Contributor   Informed   Driver

1. Decision-Maker

This is the person who advocates to actually make a particular decision. The Decision-Maker is not a recommender or an information-gatherer; rather s/he is the person who has or will be entrusted with the responsibility of making the actual decision.

2. Expert Advisor

The person who coaches the Decision-Maker to make the best decision, consulting with the Decision-Maker to provide guidance as needed. As a last resort, the advisor can also bring concerns to the executive director, if s/he is worried about the Decision-Maker's focus or abilities. There should be no more than one or two advisors per decision.

3. Contributor

This is a person who has knowledge of one or more aspects of the decision, and would like to share advice, thoughts, or concerns with the Decision-Maker. Contributors are people who should have a say in a particular decision, but are often overlooked.

In Decision Clarity, the Decision-Maker can't make a decision until s/he has consulted with everyone on its contributor list, which may entail anywhere from a five-minute chat to a lengthy series of interactions.

4. Informed

Those who need to be informed are the people who play a role in the execution of the decision, and need to be kept abreast on a timely basis so they can bring their efforts to bear on the decision. They aren't the people who merely receive the announcement email at the end of your deliberations, but rather those who need to be aware of what is happening because it may affect the decision (and their own work) in the more immediate term.

5. Driver

This optional role is used when the Decision-Maker needs additional information gathering, organizational assistance, or analytical assistance. Depending on the complexity of the decision, you may need more than one Driver. Only 10–20% of the decisions we've vetted have required this role.

BROACHING TRANSFORMATION

Whether you're an executive director, a team leader, a staff member, or a board member who wants to contribute to the transformation of your organization for the benefit of everyone involved in your nonprofit, you're likely wondering how to go about it. Depending on your role, a certain challenge lies before you in communicating your desire to the team members, and it's only natural that you may feel some degree of trepidation about presenting ideas for change. But don't let that stop you—nothing of importance ever occurs without commitment and effort; what's more, you're not alone.

In the next chapter, we'll show you exactly how to introduce Decision Clarity to your organization—whether you're the executive director, lower-level staff member, or somewhere in between—in a way that gets people excited, causes them to feel more empowered in their roles, and makes everyone feel they're contributing more positively to the cause so close to their hearts.

KEY TAKEAWAYS

Within Decision Clarity there are four process steps, represented by the acronym IPAC:

- Inventory
- Prioritize
- Advocate
- Communicate

Decision Clarity also utilizes five advocated roles, represented by the acronym D-E-C-I-D:

- Decision-Maker
- Expert Advisor
- Contributor
- Informed
- Driver

One of the many perks about the process of Decision Clarity is that it's a positive one for all involved.

A major attitudinal shift happens when people learn to advocate for the decisions they want to make or support without fear or recrimination—people want to contribute and be accountable for more while adopting a sense of empowerment.

Organizations benefit when they create unified decision-making teams for each important decision before them—a clearly identified Decision-Maker is supported by others who understand their roles as supporters.

It takes the average person no more than **15 hours** to learn and implement the four steps above.

The key deliverable is the creation of Decision Clarity grids that list all the most important decisions confronting your organization and who has advocated to make or support these decisions.

Decision Clarity grids are used as a communication tool in review meetings, board meetings, one-on-ones, and other points in time to track progress on the decisions that are moving the organization forward, unifying a team by creating visibility and clarity as to what is a priority in the organization.

6

FINDING DECISION
CLARITY ALLIES

I f you're going to make the progress you desire in your nonprofit, you'll need to recruit people to do this work with you and advance this cause. Naturally, your role in your organization dictates whom you talk to.

- ❖ If you're the executive director, you will want to talk with your board, your leadership team, and your staff.

- ❖ If you're a board member, you will want to talk with the other members of the board and your executive director.

- ❖ If you're a leader, you will want to talk with your executive director, your team, and other colleagues.

- ❖ If you're a member of the team, you will want to reach out to your leader, as well as fellow coworkers and colleagues in other parts of the organization.

Now, you may be asking: "Why, when I won't be paid extra for it and it will require some of my valuable time, should I consider making this effort?" After all, this work may initially unsettle your teammates, and you might "stir the pot." Is it worth it?

If this work reflects your values, and you believe it will help your organization achieve its mission, then your answer should be "yes."

You also want to ask yourself:

What's the worst that can happen if I do this?

What's the worst that can happen if I don't?

We think you'll see that the "worst-case scenario" is not as bad as you think; it's always better to try something new than to stick with what's not working. Not attempting to make positive change is typically much worse than swimming in circles within the status quo. Remember: Decision Clarity is a powerful tool that is simple to learn and use. Think how great you'll feel to be the catalyst of a practice that galvanizes your team in ways they didn't realize existed!

But what about resistance, you ask?

Needless to say, if you're the executive director, you can bring this practice to your organization and your team will likely embrace it. But even then, people resist change and these practices may invoke fear; you'll still have to convince people of its benefits. If you're a less senior member of the organization, you will have to network your way forward to build interest in adopting the new method and in mobilizing support (but note that the same advocacy skills you use to support your clients can be turned inward to face and improve your organization).

In short, initial resistance to change is normal, but by presenting Decision Clarity to everyone as a practice that will ultimately increase their individual sense of worth, eliminate confusion, and fortify the organization as a whole to better serve the community, you'll already be on your way to garnering support and enthusiasm.

WHO DO YOU TALK TO FIRST?

You probably know who in your organization might want to hear about Decision Clarity. Obviously, your first inclination may be to approach the individuals you feel comfortable with. This is reasonable, but it's crucial in these situations to take a comprehensive view of the people in your ecosystem. If you charge off to spread the news, you might forget an important potential ally.

Take a look at the matrix below. "Powerful" denotes people who have sway in your organization; "Friendly" denotes those who would likely be interested in this effort.

Quadrant 1	Quadrant 3
More Powerful/Friendly	More Powerful/Unfriendly
1.	1.
2.	2.
3.	3.
4.	4.
Quadrant 2	**Quadrant 4**
Less Powerful/Friendly	Less Powerful/Unfriendly
1.	1.
2.	2.
3.	3.
4.	4.

Considering the people you might approach to talk about this work, where would you place them on the grid? The best people to talk to first are those you perceive to be in Quadrant 1—these "powerful and friendly" people are most likely to support you. Perhaps your executive director or a member of the leadership team would fit into this group; maybe there's someone in your organization who doesn't have a senior rank, but because of his or her long tenure and fierce commitment to making your organization better, has a special kind of power and authority. Explore all the people who may fit into Quadrant 1 and write their names on the form.

WHO DO YOU GO TO NEXT?

Quadrant 2 represents those who are friendly but have less power. They're important allies even if they may not have a lot of positional authority. If you rally enough of these people, what they lack in individual power they can make up in mass. These are the people who may be particularly interested in advocating for decision-making that affects their jobs.

Quadrant 3 is composed of those you perceive to be "unfriendly and powerful"—this is the most daunting category. Depending on the level of enthusiasm you garner from those in Quadrants 1 and 2, you may be able to recruit additional allies to aid you in speaking with these people. If you have the members of this third quadrant pegged right, they will probably have the most resistance to making changes in your organization's decision-making processes—with a significant need for control and less interest in allowing people to advocate to make or support the decisions that are key to their jobs. But just because these people may be resistant doesn't mean that you can or should avoid them. After all, your biases about their interest may be incorrect.

If you believe the people in this quadrant are committed to achieving your organization's mission, engage them. Explain why you're interested in this approach and how the organization will benefit. Don't run from these people; they may become allies to help you make the case if you present a message they find compelling. There's always the possibility that these people can transition into Quadrant 1 allies and be of real service to advancing the goal of clarifying power and decision-making in your organization.

Last, Quadrant 4 contains those who would be unfriendly and have little power. We advise you to ignore these people for the time being; they probably can't or won't help you in the beginning. But if you succeed in getting Decision Clarity implemented in your organization, they will likely come along and become as enthusiastic about it as you are.

The point here is that in order to get Decision Clarity moving in your organization— especially if you aren't the executive director—you'll have to gain the agreement of as many senior and/or influential people as possible. If you can't convince anyone to move forward, you can always use the tools and skills you've learned to advocate for more decision-making clarity for yourself. But the more people you can bring into the circle, the greater the impact you can foster. Aim high, think positively, and be audacious.

TEST THE WATER WITH A FEW QUESTIONS

As we've discussed, people often believe they don't have the power to shape their decision-making ecosystem—that the way it is now is the way it has to be forever. Programs evolve, policies change, organizations shift their missions, but decision-making habits and practices appear to be impossible to change. People don't even know that they can question these practices, so they often don't. But once you've decided you want to advance this method, and you've done your "ally analysis," it's time to begin the process of gathering support.

We know it's difficult to talk about realigning power and decision-making, and often people don't know what to say to open the conversation, so we've provided you some language to help you in your effort. As asking others to enter into a conversation about power and decision-making can render you tongue-tied and anxious, these suggestions are designed to help you lessen your anxiety. If, by chance, you know what you want to say and don't need assistance, that's super! However, if you're uncertain, you can rely on the following guidance.

We recommend that you meet with the first Quadrant-1 person on your list, and begin with some variation of the following statement:

"I've recently read a book that I've enjoyed, and I want to share some of its principles with you. It examines issues of power and decision-making in nonprofit organizations. I know we don't usually talk about how decisions are made in our organization, but it's an important topic to discuss. But before I get into the book, I wonder if I could ask you a few questions." (Pick two or three that are relevant to your organization from the list below.)

1. Do you feel you have the opportunity to make the important decisions that affect your job?

2. Looking at our organization, do you think we're clear enough about all the decisions we have to make and who makes them?

3. Do you have time to focus on all the decisions you have to make?

4. Do you sometimes feel that you're overwhelmed with too many decisions to make?

5. Do you think we waste time and money because we're unclear who will be making what decisions?

6. Do you think we waste time and money because we revisit decisions?

7. Do we have bottlenecks that slow decision-making?

8. Do you think we're so consensus-driven that it's difficult for us to make decisions?

9. Do you think we can use more of our team to make the decisions that confront us?

10. Do you think we lose people to other organizations because we don't allow or enable them to make decisions that affect their jobs?

After asking a few of these questions, you will most likely find that your conversation partner reveals plenty about how your organization's decision-making practices currently function. Nonprofits typically have numerous issues around this topic, so it would be a rare organization that did not demonstrate some form of challenge. With the answers to these questions in mind, you can now launch into your advocacy for Decision Clarity.

DIVE IN: THE MESSAGE

Using the following as a guide, but tailoring it to you, consider these words when moving forward with your conversation:

"The book I mentioned talks about a concept called "Decision Clarity," and it really got me excited. Imagine how great it would be if every member of our team began each day with a full understanding of the decisions that they need to make to advance the mission of our organization with no confusion or conflict. We would already know which decisions we're empowered to make and which decisions others are making. And as new ones pop up, we have a process and a language for talking about who will make them.

"One of the greatest benefits of this method is a shared process and language that will increase our decision-making focus. But the biggest benefit is that it enables us to use the resources we already have to become more concentrated and to achieve more. We don't have to hire additional people or spend money on expensive technology because we'll be using the underutilized abilities of the people who are already in our organization to move us forward.

"By using this practice, everyone will have increased focus on the decisions that are central to their jobs, and we'll develop more people who can make decisions, which will create a healthier, more effective workplace. Because people are more engaged and are given increased opportunities to make decisions, they will grow in their jobs and stay longer. This will cut our recruiting costs and increase our effectiveness because we won't have to replace our employees as often.

"One of the best parts is that it only takes a few hours of commitment from each person to make an exponential difference in our organization. [The person will likely be surprised when you say this.] Does this sound like something you'd be interested in being part of?"

Remember, your colleagues are likely just as tired as you are, so it's critical to paint a picture for them. They may have little faith that anything can be done to improve how your organization works; their philosophy may even be "grin and bear it." So speak to the fact that you have this clear and comprehensive process that will actually make a difference.

Once you're finished, move on to the next person in Quadrant 1 and so on, through your Quadrant 2 list. Unless your presentation is endorsed by a number of senior Quadrant-1 people, the campaign for Decision Clarity may take a while. But don't be discouraged. People need time to assimilate new ideas, and you can engage them in an open process.

How Might People Respond?

There are a number of ways that those you approach may respond. It's important for you to be prepared for these responses and to have your own follow-up statements. Here are the most common ones.

1

Obviously, this is the best possible answer. Think through with this person how you can introduce Decision Clarity into his or her area, and then how you can rally people to support the idea. Reinforce that this is a focused and time-efficient program—it will take some time to orchestrate it, but if it's done right, the initial setup will save much more time than is expended. This response signifies good news and is a major achievement. Congratulations on your effort!

2

These people might have a genuine interest in Decision Clarity but may require more information. If this is the case, recommend the book to them and direct them to www.scheiergroup.com where they can learn more about the benefits of the work.

There's also a chance that these people may not want to pursue or support this effort but are unwilling to say so for fear of offending you, so ask specifically what they will need to decide on supporting this initiative. If you provide the requested information and they are still uncertain, move on to the next person on your list.

3

You may encounter people who are enthusiastic or at least open to the principles you've laid out, but simply can't make the effort a priority. The short-term pressure to get tasks done overshadows the time to pursue an initiative that can actually *save* time and effort in the long run. Remind people who respond this way that while it will take some time to mobilize the team and implement the method, clarifying decision-making in your organization will save far more time than what is expended. Make the argument and see what they say. These people may be genuinely interested but simply need some time to think about it, so be compassionate and ask them to provide you with a specific time window to revisit the subject.

4

Clarity and honesty are universally good—even when the answer may not be what you want. Some people may simply not be interested, or think it's too risky to inject something new into what they may consider a precarious organizational climate. If this is the answer you receive, be sure to get this person to share his or her reasons, being as specific as possible. Perhaps this person has had a bad experience that s/he can speak to. Perhaps power was wrested from him or her in another job. Perhaps this person is falling victim to implicit bias about how organizations should work.

There are many reasons people initially say "no." Unless the person is agitated about the conversation for some reason, hang in there a bit. Ask why s/he has this perspective and whether you could provide insights that might change his or her mind. If the response remains consistent, thank the person for their time and move on. Still, don't be afraid to ask people who say "no" to elaborate on their feelings. It may actually benefit both of you.

KEEP TALKING

If you've had a successful interaction, take your enthusiasm to the next person. If your first meeting didn't go well, ask yourself how you can improve your approach. Keep in mind that people may need to hear things several times, and that each person brings his or her own baggage to any conversation; they may each communicate and hear things differently. But the great thing is that the Decision Clarity philosophy will appeal to many people as you continue to speak about it.

If you're the executive director of your organization, you can probably bring this practice to your team with little outward resistance, but you will still have to sell it. Even with the power you have, people will want to know why they should participate in this effort, and how they and the organization will benefit from doing so. People feel very protective of their time; they look at their to-do lists all day long and often feel over-burdened. Even if they see an opportunity for benefit, most people approach change warily. And the promise of greater decision-making clarity may not be compelling for those who are risk-averse and prone to keeping things predictable—even when the status quo isn't necessarily good for the organization.

This is why it's important to emphasize the benefits each person—as well as the organization—will receive. Let's be honest: even in the face of change, it's difficult to reject the idea of feeling better about your job, having say in the issues you desire, and being respected for the talent and ideas you can bring to the table, not to mention being able to more effectively serve the community you love so much.

GENERAL MOBILIZATION TECHNIQUES

After you complete your initial set of one-on-one interviews and you have buy-in from your organization, you can use other tools to bring Decision Clarity to your organization. Here are some suggestions:

1. **Give a formal presentation.**

   Share with your team the details of the method and benefits of Decision Clarity.

2. **Create a book discussion session.**

   Encourage people in your organization to read the book, and then lead a discussion group. Delve into how your organization can benefit from implementing the Decision Clarity practice.

3. **Use social media to spread the word in your nonprofit.**

   Post updates on what you're doing with Decision Clarity on Twitter, Facebook, LinkedIn, Instagram, or other outlets.

A WORD ON BOARD/EXECUTIVE DIRECTOR INTERACTIONS

If you're an executive director, you may want to bring Decision Clarity to your board, but you might wonder whether it's worth it to break with your board's established pattern of operation. Ask yourself the following questions:

❖ Are you getting the most you can from your board?

❖ Does your board make the decisions you need them to make?

❖ Do they encroach on decisions you think are clearly within your purview?

❖ Does your board micromanage and involve themselves in topics that are, from your perspective, outside their scope?

❖ Is your board checked out and only taking action when you prod them?

❖ Does your board keep their commitments?

❖ Have you tried to delineate a division of power and decision-making responsibilities to your board? If so, what happened?

❖ Does your board know what roles you want them to play in the decisions you make?

❖ How much time did you and your board waste in the last year discussing issues where it was unclear who would actually make the decision you were debating?

❖ Does your board focus on "safe topics," or is it fully engaged in helping you move your organization forward?

❖ Are you happy with the decision-making focus of your board?

Your answers to these questions will be telling. As you consider them, you may begin to see opportunities for further clarity between you and your board.

Because you're at the helm of decision-making in your organization, you will be well served to understand which decisions your board wants to make and which you want to make. We recognize that most boards and executive directors would rather not address hard topics, but clarifying power and decision-making with your board will be extremely beneficial in the long run.

At the same time, if you're a board member, you may be thinking about how you can use Decision Clarity to work more effectively with your executive director, but you might wonder whether it's worth changing the dynamic of your interactions. You may likewise feel the pressure of your fiduciary and governance responsibilities without being clear on what you can and cannot do. While some board members believe their attendance at board meetings is sufficient, many are deeply interested in the missions of their organizations but aren't sure how to maximize their involvement without stepping on toes. Board service is not an easy task, and it can be made more complicated by strong executive directors who won't let their board pierce the veil of their operations, or by weak executive directors who allow their boards to amass too much decision-making responsibility.

If you're a board member, ask yourself the following questions:

- How many times do you leave your board meeting feeling like you've wasted your time?

- Does your executive director readily share the important metrics being pursued by the organization, or does s/he hide behind generalities?

- Have you clarified which decisions the board will make and which will fall to your executive director?

- Does your executive director come to you to ask for your input on specific decisions s/he is going to make?

- How many important decisions has the board made in the past year? Are you focused on the most important decisions or are there decisions you're ducking?

- How much time do you waste debating issues when you're unclear who will actually make the decision you're discussing?

- Are you happy with the decision-making focus of the board and the organization you serve?

If the answers to these questions give you pause, you have an excellent reason for discussing the advantages of Decision Clarity with your executive director and how you would like to use the method to clarify power and decision-making between you. As you explain your ideas to your colleagues, be sure to illuminate that the current and future state of decision-making in your organization will save time, money, and frustration—it's rare for someone to dispute that!

BE THE CHANGE

As Gandhi said, "You must be the change you want to see in the world." Advocating for transformation requires a significant commitment, and because everyone in the nonprofit sector is busy and has a lot to do, if you indeed decide that this practice is important to your organization, you'll have to carve out some time from your busy day to advance it. Be patient and don't get discouraged if it takes a while to achieve critical mass in your organization; everything worthwhile requires time and effort to accomplish it.

While it can be daunting to visualize how to start a conversation about power and decision-making in your organization, the good news is that nonprofit organizations and their leadership are filled with people who seek to advance a mission beyond their own narrow interests. Sure, there are those who will seek to maintain their own power and control. But most nonprofits have boards, leadership, and staff who are mission-focused, innovative, and willing to try new approaches to making their organizations more effective.

Many nonprofit leaders want to build inclusive environments where their employees can make a difference but simply don't know how. You can be the person who points the way.

LET'S DO IT!

Regardless of your role, you are now ready to contribute to the transformation of your organization for the benefit of everyone involved in your nonprofit. Some of the activities you will do individually, and others you will perform with your colleagues, but overall, it's a social activity that is best advanced through working with others—a method designed for people to engage each other in the issues of power and decision-making without fear of recrimination or guilt. As you work through these next chapters, you will imagine a world where bottlenecks cease to exist, and you will see the concrete ways the full capabilities of you and your team can be realized.

KEY TAKEAWAYS

Decision Clarity is a powerful tool that is simple to learn and use.

You can use the provided scripts as a guideline for your conversations to minimize fear and enhance confidence.

You'll talk to the "Powerful and Friendly" first to garner allies for early support—even if you're unsure whether they will endorse the practice—then move on to other members outlined in the "Who to Talk To" matrix.

You can use the Decision Clarity concepts in your own work as a way to model the process and what it can do; in short, you can be the person who points the way!

If it feels daunting to attempt change, remember that most nonprofits have boards, leadership, and staff who are mission-focused, innovative, and willing to try new approaches to making their organizations more effective.

If you're an executive director, clarifying power and decision-making with your board is always extremely beneficial in the long run; it is likewise valuable for boards to do the same with their executive director.

Even when they see opportunity for improvement, most people are overburdened and approach change warily, which is why it's crucial to emphasize the benefits each person—as well as the organization—will receive from adopting the practice.

7

STEP ONE:
INVENTORYING DECISIONS

Have you ever taken the time to inventory the decisions that affect your job? If you're like most people, you keep a short list of *tasks* in your head, but few people are deliberate enough to take stock of their actual *decisions* (but you will be shortly).

As an example of the power of this simple process, consider GreatSchools[8], a prominent Oakland, CA-based nonprofit. Bill Jackson and Matthew Nelson (the CEO and COO respectively) recognized that too many decisions were falling to them, and they wanted to involve more of their team. After engaging us to work with their organization, we met with the entire 65-person staff in a series of team meetings and had them list the decisions before them.

After the first round, we presented the comprehensive decision inventory list to Bill. There were more than 80 high-impact decisions on the list, and about 25% had not previously surfaced in the organization's day-to-day discussions. This was a revelation to Bill and Matthew. After shedding light on all the influential decisions that their fast-paced and growing organization had to make, the team felt more empowered to move forward with clarity and confidence—in short, to do more good, better.

---

[8] GreatSchools "is the leading national source of parenting information, reaching 60 million unique visitors and 50% of American families with children." (from www.GreatSchools.com)

WHAT IS A DECISION INVENTORY?

A decision inventory is simply a list of the decisions that you want or need to make (or support). This list is *not* framed in the language of strategic plans or objectives, but is instead a descriptive, granular list of the crucial decisions that make a difference to you and your organization.

Decision Inventory

The Decision to Create a:
- Fundraiser
- Marketing Plan
- Policy Paper
- Program Plan
- Volunteer Training

Here is a sample of a real decision inventory from our engagement with the Zen Hospice Project:

Sample Decision Inventory

1. Decide which updates/modifications to new volunteer training we want to do
2. Determine what other sites/agencies would benefit from hosting our caregiver volunteers
3. Who should present at volunteer community meetings in 2014
4. How to create a volunteer advisory council
5. Go/no-go on spring volunteer training
6. When to do the spring volunteer caregiver training

7.   Create a plan on how to best manage Guest House kitchen

8.   Create a plan to engage Guest House volunteers fully on their shifts

9.   Create a plan for a Guest House ongoing family support program

10. Create a plan to determine whether or not to let LHH-S3 volunteers begin serving as substitutes at Guest House

11. Create a plan to relaunch volunteer council with specific structure and goals

12. Create a plan on managing volunteers at LHH and Guest House after March 1, 2014

There are three general categories of decisions in a decision inventory:

❖   Those that are well-articulated and easy to capture, because you know you need to make them (e.g., Go/no-go on spring volunteer training).

❖   Those that are broad because you're just starting a project and haven't gotten deep enough to know what direction you're taking (e.g., Create a plan for a GH ongoing family support program).

❖   Those that are in your area, and you'd *like* to be making them, but you may not feel empowered to do so (e.g., Create a plan to determine whether or not to let LHH-S3 volunteers begin serving as substitutes at Guest House).

In this chapter, each person on your staff will be creating two inventories. The first will represent the present state of your decision-making—or what is currently on your plate. The second will ask you to imagine your future state of decision-making—or what you'd ideally like to focus on. For now, we simply want you to get your ideas down. In Chapter 10, we'll become more specific with the language.

Your first two lists are practice inventories, so don't worry about the practical aspects yet; inventorying decisions is an act of reflection, not action. As you build proficiency in this skill, you will ready yourself to make your final Decision Clarity Grid (in Chapter 10).

WHY CREATE A DECISION INVENTORY?

The benefits of inventorying your decisions are four-fold.

1. Shift Your Thinking

Nonprofit leaders and staff have been acculturated into thinking that by creating objectives, strategies, plans, and tactics, they will move their organization forward.

While not misguided, these actions are not the whole story. What is often missing in these actions is a mutually recognized agreement on *who* is actually making the decisions that will determine the success of these objectives, strategies, plans, and tactics. Listing your decisions in advance is the first step toward this new way of thinking.

2. Limit Confusion and Create More Focus for the Conversation

By listing your decisions in as much granularity as possible, you find places where you've made assumptions and/or places where you may have missed important dependencies.

3. Build the Habit of Proactively Approaching Decision-Making

In our 2010 study on decision-making with Commongood Careers, we asked the respondents whether their organizations tried to proactively determine the decisions they could make. A whopping 81% of staff and 68% of managers answered in the negative. These results proved that we are typically not good at understanding who will make which decisions, and this has costly consequences for everyone in our organizations.

4. Remove Bottlenecks in Your Organization

When nonprofit leaders focus their efforts on a smaller set of decisions that have high impact and drive the rest to other qualified people in their organizations, bottlenecks are eliminated.

And there is an added benefit: when executive directors, in particular, create their first decision inventories, they often see (for the first time) the totality of the decisions that they either want to make, feel they *have* to make, or believe they are *expected* to make. Executive directors also see the decisions that simply default to them, either because staff isn't clear about who has the deciding authority, or because no one believes they can advocate for decision-making power.

WHAT TO EXPECT

Completing your "current state" inventory is always a sobering experience. If you're an executive director, you may come face to face with the sheer volume of decisions you're called upon to make. If you're a board member, leader, or staff person, you may be surprised at all the decisions on your plate too. Additionally, you may see a pattern where decisions that don't have an actual owner either languish or simply default to the executive director. You will also see clearly what's not within your purview that you think should officially be there.

When you create a decision inventory with the other members of your team, you will likely encounter some interesting dynamics. For example, when a team is unclear as to who should make a particular decision, and they see their leader weighing in on all decisions—large and small—they assume the leader is the default decision-maker. As a result of this unstated agreement, staff will continue to drive decision-making to their leader (even when encouraged to do otherwise).

Watch for these established patterns in the initial inventorying phase, marking your assumptions about the power you have and don't have. Be mindful also of which decisions you "automatically" assume are yours (if you're the executive director), or are not yours (if you're leadership or staff).

CREATING YOUR DECISION INVENTORY

The following activities are designed to have you dispassionately look at the decisions you make (in your current state), and to explore what a future state may look like.

Inventory Activity 1:

How many work decisions do you make every month?

You make more decisions than you think. Studies vary, but it's been suggested that humans make hundreds of decisions each day. In order to get a good sample of your current decision-making focus, consider the decisions you have made at work over the last month. Note: Don't list decisions that were arrived at by "consensus," but ones that you personally made. Here is some language you can use:

This past month, I decided to_____.

Write your decisions in the space below:

1.

2.

3.

4.

5.

6.

7.

8.

9.

10.

11.

12.

13.

14.

Inventory Activity 2:
What are the *important* decisions you've made?

This next activity is designed to get you in the habit of thinking about the importance of your decisions. We will give you more specific guidance on how to prioritize decisions in the next chapter, but for now, simply list the decisions you believe are important to you and your organization. At this point, we'll give you a great deal of latitude in how you define *important*.

Here are examples of crucial decisions that nonprofit staff make every day. Feel free to use the list below to guide your reflection.

- ❖ which funders to approach for support

- ❖ how to deliver your organization's program model

- ❖ how large your operating budget should grow for the upcoming fiscal year

- ❖ which events will be produced to advance your efforts

- ❖ what messages to include in your communication strategy

- ❖ how to use social media to promote your organization

- ❖ how many and which staff your organization hires

- ❖ how to recruit and manage your volunteers

- ❖ who is eligible to participate in your program

- ❖ what goals should be established for your strategic plan

- ❖ who should be recruited for board service

- ❖ how to best control organizational expenses

You'll note these decisions always begin with which, how, who, and what (and sometimes "when" or "why"). As the famed sculptor Michelangelo once said, "Every block of stone has a statue inside it and it is the task of the sculptor to discover it."

Decisions written at a granular level are the hidden treasure (statue) in the block of stone (your organization's objectives, strategies, plans, and tactics). Decisions live inside these elements, and your challenge is to carve out and list the *important* ones that sit in your head, your laptop, your bookshelf, and the pile on your desk.

So let's widen the timeframe of this activity, and narrow the focus of your decision-making by thinking about the past year and listing the important decisions you have made at work. Here is some language you can use:

Over the last year, I made the following important decisions for my nonprofit:

1.

2.

3.

4.

5.

6.

7.

8.

9.

10.

11.

12.

13.

14.

Inventory Activity 3
Questions for Your Future State

In the prior two activities, you created a general list of the decisions you've made, and then a more targeted list of those that were important. These lists give you some indication of the current state of your decision-making focus.

Now, let's take a comprehensive look at both of these inventories and consider the following questions:

❖ What are the important decisions I want to continue to make?

❖ What are the important decisions I no longer want to make?

❖ What are the important decisions I want to start making?

❖ Which are decisions that cause confusion and that I'm not sure who is ultimately making?

Write down your answers, and don't stop until you have at least three or four responses in each category. If you're having trouble coming up with decisions for each of these categories, ask a trusted friend or colleague for advice.

The reason it's vital to form an understanding of your "current state" of decision-making is to give you the space to begin thinking about the "future state" you want to achieve by the end of the Decision Clarity process.

Now we want you to consider the question: What stands out from your self-assessment? Use the space below to write at least three sentences on what you learned from these activities. Take note of how you felt about the experience. Do you believe that your decision-making capabilities are over-utilized or underutilized in your organization? Do you feel trusted to make decisions in your ecosystem?

Your New Insight

It is our hope that these activities have shed light on the current state of your decision-making responsibility and allowed you to think more broadly about decisions you may want to divest yourself of or want to start making.

By investing this short amount of time in your inventory, you've taken the first step in thinking about *decisions*, rather than the objectives, strategies, plans, and tactics you are typically immersed in. In the next chapter, we'll master the skill of prioritizing decisions, taking you one step closer to transforming your organization for the better.

KEY TAKEAWAYS

Creating decision inventories allows you to take stock of all the key decisions you or someone else has to make to advance your organization.

Decision inventories shift individual thinking by forcing participants to think of the granular decisions they have to make so they are no longer embedded in plans and strategies.

Decision inventories limit confusion and create more focus for decision-makers, while encouraging *proactive* rather than *reactive* decision-making.

Inventories call out decision-making bottlenecks and reveal where people are overloaded and stymied.

People often focus on less important decisions because the more critical ones may prove to be controversial.

Inventorying decisions creates calm and reduces anxiety by allowing the participants to "get their arms around" the decision-making challenges they face.

STEP TWO:
PRIORITIZING DECISIONS

It should come as no surprise that not all decisions are created equal. When we interview executive directors for our engagements, we ask them to tell us their organizational vision for the next five years. Most are capable of explaining where they want to take their organizations and how they want to impact the social challenge they are tackling. But when we ask them *how much time* they actually devote to the decisions that will advance their vision, their answer is almost always, "not enough."

Sound familiar? For many nonprofit leaders, decisions can feel almost like tidal waves. There's the existing surge of current decisions, and then waves of new decisions arrive in the form of questions, comments, requests, and demands. These new waves come from both inside (current donors, clients, staff, board members) and outside (new donors, new clients, the press, political leaders), and each can appear suddenly and threaten to drench everything.

So how do you keep your head above water and navigate where to put your time?

You prioritize. And chances are you already have a prioritizing scheme you're using —whether it is conscious or not. For example, some people look at decisions they need to make through the prism of "Who will I please?" or "Who will I disappoint?" Others focus on the decisions that are the easiest and quickest to resolve. Still others attend simply to the issue that is most urgent, falling prey to the trap of dealing with whatever is most public and pressing, whether it's actually important or not. There are many methods for prioritizing, and they all work as a lens to focus your time and attention, but we will teach you a particular mode of prioritizing that will best serve you as a nonprofit leader or member of the team.

MAINTENANCE VS. HIGH-IMPACT DECISIONS

In our work with nonprofits, we look at decisions in terms of maintenance and high-impact. Maintenance decisions are inescapable—deciding on a payroll service, what kind of office supplies you should buy, or what a donor thank-you letter should say all fall into this category. Depending on the size of your nonprofit, there may be hundreds of maintenance decisions made every day in your organization.

To be clear, maintenance decisions are **not**, by definition, unimportant. Choosing the right payroll service so you can pay your people on time is certainly a crucial decision to make; procuring the right deal on office supplies is also important; the content of your donor thank-you letters is likewise critical. These are all maintenance decisions because they don't likely require the decision-maker to establish a new framework. What's more, the costs of making a poor maintenance decision, while perhaps initially damaging, are usually recoverable. Most can be made without strife or rancor, and without comment or controversy, with minimal complexity and little emotion attached to them.

High-impact decisions, in contrast, are those that have significant financial, pro-grammatic, relationship, organizational, or political ramifications. These are what you may consider the "scary" decisions, those that can do significant damage if mishandled, yet can create tremendous benefit if done right. A few examples would be deciding which new populations to serve, whether or not to expand (or contract) operations, or forging a partnership with another organization. Obviously, these decisions tend to have some form of emotion or conflict associated with them, and they are usually more complex.

As high-impact decisions are crucial to moving your organization forward and are the ones that will define whether your organization and its mission will flourish or languish, they also tend to be less frequent. But just because the decisions in this category are relatively few in number (compared to the omnipresent maintenance category), they customarily demand significant attention.

What's curious to note is that it's easy to make every maintenance decision under the sun and not devote the necessary time to the high-impact decisions that will make a true difference to your organization. Conversely, it's actually impossible to focus solely on high-impact decisions, because we typically don't have this luxury. Therefore, prioritizing decisions is about increasing your high-impact decision-making *ratio*. It's about gaining increased focus on the decisions that matter, and encouraging others to do the same.

A WORD ABOUT POWER

When you make the distinction between maintenance and high-impact decisions, you may notice that issues of power arise. Some leaders will unconsciously focus on the total number of decisions before them, and make their goal a simple reduction of that number. In other words, their prioritization method is to simply tick things off their list.

People using this system can easily make the quantity-over-quality argument, which sounds something like, "It's not my fault that I couldn't get everything done and that I didn't have time to perform due diligence on these important decisions—look at all I had to do." Note that the tone of this argument is about who or what is to blame. When people don't feel they have made an explicit agreement to make a particular decision, they will often (understandably) defend themselves after the fact. In addition, when they don't feel empowered to make the important, high-impact decisions, they will content themselves with comparatively safe maintenance decisions.

The effects of power can also work in reverse. If nonprofit leaders feel unable to divest themselves of maintenance decisions (can't or won't delegate), they won't be able to justify spending time on more important, high-impact decisions. Issues of power are always present when deciding what gets priority and what doesn't, so be on the watch for how power comes into play as you begin exploring prioritization.

PRIORITIZING IN ACTION

In this step of the Decision Clarity practice, we encourage you to take stock of the nature of the decisions you make and to consider whether you need to shift the ratio of your decision-making in the high-impact direction in subtle ways, or more dramatically.

If you change your own ratio, the shift will set the stage for allowing others in your ecosystem to do the same. This will result in more focus on the decisions that make a difference, and more candid discussions about decisions that take up a lot of time, yet don't reap real benefits. The skill of prioritizing helps you focus, and having more focus will create better decision-making. Focus is what we're after.

In the previous chapter, we discussed the necessity of taking stock of all the decisions that affect your job. In this chapter we're going to tease out which are the important decisions you should focus on. This *isn't* a process where you will put in rank order all the decisions that *everyone else* wants you to make; rather, this is about establishing a list of the decisions that, *from your perspective*, are the most critical for you to make.

Prioritizing Activity 1:

Your Current Ratio

To get a sense of your current decision ratio (maintenance vs. high-impact decisions), we've created a matrix to help you map it out. For the purposes of this activity, a difficult decision is one that has many "moving parts" and has to be considered carefully; an easy decision has few "moving parts" and can be considered quickly.

As mentioned before, a *maintenance* decision is one that is important but is a regular part of running a business. It can be made without strife. A *high-impact* decision, in contrast, is one that has significant financial, programmatic, relationship, organizational, or political ramifications and is crucial for moving your organization forward. An *easy* high-impact decision might be whether to accept an unexpected donation from a highly desirable source. A *difficult* high-impact decision might be whether to merge with a similar organization in another part of the state.

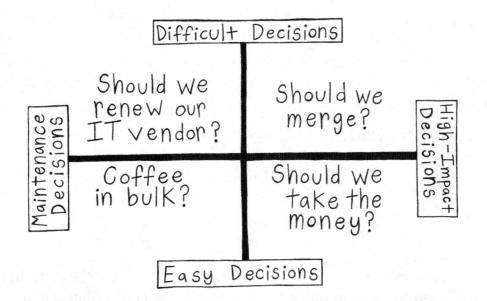

Taking your list from Activity #1 in Chapter 7 (pp. 144–45), plot the decisions on the matrix below:

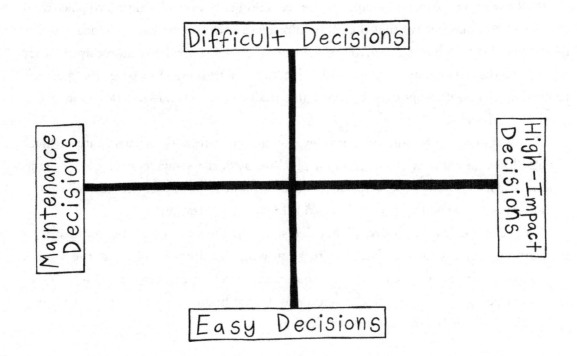

What do you notice?

Where do most of your decisions currently fall?

This matrix paints a picture of where you're spending your time. Certainly the more senior you are in an organization, the more time you should be spending in the high-impact category. If you have a leadership role in your organization, and most of your decisions aren't in the high-impact category, you're either not being permitted the latitude to perform your job, or you're simply not focused on the right decisions.

And where on the matrix would you expect middle- or entry-level staff to place their decisions? You may believe that they should primarily occupy the maintenance decision quadrants, that they haven't earned the right to make high-impact decisions, or that they don't have the appropriate background, education, or training. We pose this question right now because it's important to reveal any bias you may have. (We'll talk more about bias in Chapter 11.)

Think about it: if middle- or entry-level staff aren't allowed to participate in high-impact decisions, how can you create a pipeline of decision-makers for your organization? And if they don't have a chance to make even one high-impact decision relevant to their positions, how will you grow these skills in your organization?

Now let's look at the board. What decisions do they make? Is the board micro-managing to such a degree that they're approving the floral displays at the annual fundraiser, or are they focused on the important governance decisions before them? Have the leaders been clear with the board about what high-impact decisions they are to make? Has the board been clear with the leadership?

All of these questions are designed to get you thinking about how your organization spends its time, and how you can make distinctions around decisions and communicate them to others. More importantly, these questions ask you to consider how many low-impact decisions you or your organization are spending the time to make, and whether those are the best use of your talents and time.

LONG-TERM CHALLENGE

Over the next month, we urge you to keep a record of the high-impact and maintenance decisions you make. If you're like most people, your maintenance decisions will significantly outnumber the high-impact ones. As you write down these decisions, make notes about where you get drawn into maintenance mode, and how that happens. Try to pay attention to what internal processes you use to decide what gets priority, and how you're using your decision-making time.

DECISION PRIORITIZATION AT WORK

As mentioned in the previous chapter, during our GreatSchools engagement, the 65 staff members participating in the workshop initially inventoried more than 80 high-impact decisions. They also (surprisingly) asserted that their CEO, Bill Jackson, should retain decision-making authority on more than 30 of these decisions.

When Bill saw this list, he was aghast. Even though he had previously discussed with his team the value of driving decision-making authority down into the organization, his staff's initial instinct was to reinforce *his* responsibilities and not support their own. Over the succeeding days, Bill whittled the list of the high-impact decisions he was willing to make from more than 30 to just six. Seeing all of those decisions in black and white was jarring, and to Bill's credit, he realized he had to focus—which is exactly what he did.

DECISION FATIGUE

Focusing the majority of attention on high-impact decisions not only makes good organizational sense, but it also makes good biological sense. Scientific research has shown that humans only have the capacity to make a finite number of decisions over a given period. Our ability to make decisions erodes as the day goes on, and the more decisions we feel we have to make, the more drained we become. Our decision-making capacities are not an inexhaustible resource, so it's vital to know how to prioritize. *New York Times* science columnist John Tierney writes about this phenomenon[9].

> No matter how rational and high-minded you try to be, you can't make decision after decision without paying a biological price. It's different from ordinary physical fatigue—you're not consciously aware of being tired—but you're low on mental energy. The more choices you make throughout the day, the harder each one becomes for your brain, and eventually it looks for shortcuts, usually in either of two very different ways. One shortcut is to become reckless: to act impulsively instead of expending energy to first think through the consequences. The other shortcut is the ultimate energy saver: do nothing. Instead of agonizing over decisions, avoid any choice. Ducking a decision often creates bigger problems in the long run, but for the moment it eases mental strain ... As a result, you start to resist any change, any potentially risky move ...

Do you find too many decisions on your plate? If so, you're at risk of decision fatigue unless you find a way to parcel out some of your responsibility in this arena. You can combat decision fatigue through prioritization. When decisions come to leaders, we suggest that they ask the following questions:

❖ Is this a decision someone in our organization should make?

❖ If so, which member of the team is best equipped to make it?

❖ If not, how can we be direct about *not* pursuing this decision?

---

[9] "Do You Suffer from Decision Fatigue?" *New York Times*, August 17, 2011.

Being deliberate and direct about what gets priority and what doesn't is the first way to combat decision fatigue. The following activities are designed to have you practice prioritizing and consider what a more streamlined decision-making focus might look and feel like.

Prioritizing Activity 2:

Three Decisions That Could Make a Difference

To practice the skill of prioritizing, review your results from Activity 1, and think about three high-impact decisions you could make that would help you and your organization move closer to achieving your mission. Are these decisions already on your list? They may be, or they may not be.

Perhaps you haven't had permission to "dream" about impact in this way. Maybe you've been avoiding these decisions because the timing isn't right (or the idea provokes a bit of fear in you). Perhaps you simply haven't had time to consider the question fully. In any case, whether you're unclear, afraid, or enthusiastically open to moving forward, now is the time to name the decisions on the next page.

Once again, a high-impact decision is one that has significant financial, program-matic, relationship, organizational, or political ramifications, is usually complex, and is crucial for moving your organization forward.

The top three high-impact decisions I can make to advance my organization's mission are:

The decision to:

The decision to:

The decision to:

How does it feel to have named these decisions? Do you feel fear? Uncertainty? Inspiration? Confidence? Make a note of this.

Prioritizing Activity 3:
Decisions to Give Up

Next, we'll use the important decisions list you created in Activity 2 in Chapter 7 (p. 147) to prepare you for the next step of the Decision Clarity practice—advocating. Assuming you've embraced that focus and prioritization are important to you and your organization's ability to be more effective, the next logical question is:

❖   Which decisions warrant your decision-making focus?

Consider your matrix from Activity 1 in this chapter—if you're like most people, you have too many maintenance decisions, not enough high-impact decisions, or too many overall decisions. The bottom line is, something's got to give. In order to gain more focus, you'll have to either cut back on the decisions you make, or allow others to make them. A third option is to no longer address, or sharply curtail, decisions that are detracting from your mission. Every decision should be able to withstand the test of whether it is actually relevant now, or will be in the future.

Given where you want to focus your decision-making:

❖ What are the decisions you are willing to give to others?

❖ What are the decisions that no longer make sense for you to be making, or for your organization to be considering?

I am willing to give the following decisions to others:

The decision to:

The decision to:

The decision to:

The decision to:

The decision to:

The decision to:

The decision to:

The decision to:

The decision to:

The decision to:

I am willing to advocate that we eliminate the following decisions from the organization:

The decision to:

The decision to:

The decision to:

The decision to:

The decision to:

The decision to:

The decision to:

The decision to:

The decision to:

The decision to:

The decision to:

Prioritizing Activity 4:

Decisions That Merit New Decision-Makers

Depending on your role in your organization, you may find that there are decisions you would like to be responsible for but are not permitted to make (or the decisions do not have clear ownership). These are rarely directly addressed in nonprofits, but you may have a vested interest in considering them.

Given where you want to focus your decision-making, what are the decisions you would like to assume responsibility for (but are not allowed to make at this time)?

I would like to make the following decisions:

The decision to:

The decision to:

The decision to:

The decision to:

The decision to:

Given where you want to focus your decision-making, what clarity do you need on who is currently responsible?

I would like clarity on who is making the following decisions:

The decision to:

The decision to:

The decision to:

The decision to:

Prioritizing Activity 5:
Summing It Up

Now that you've examined the inventory of your important decisions in detail, identified your top three high-impact decisions, and determined the decisions you want to give to others (and possibly ones you want to include in your sphere of responsibility), it's time to summarize your newly prioritized list.

Top 3 high-impact decisions I want to make and can make:

The decision to:

The decision to:

The decision to:

Decisions I want to give to others:

The decision to:

The decision to:

The decision to:

New decisions I want the responsibility to make:

The decision to:

The decision to:

The decision to:

Decisions I want clarity on:

The decision to:

The decision to:

The decision to:

This will not be the final list you use to create your Decision Clarity grid in Chapter 10, but having practiced the skill of prioritizing will serve you well when you're ready to perform this step. Consider these final questions:

❖ Is prioritizing easy for you?

❖ If not, why is it difficult?

❖ What is the hardest part of this skill for you to master?

THE ULTIMATE BENEFIT OF PRIORITIZING

By this point, you should have a thorough understanding of what's on your decision plate, and where you have an opportunity to focus more time and attention. You should also have a sense of your natural prioritizing skills, and what kind of filters you want to use.

But what is the ultimate benefit of prioritizing? In his book, *Focus: The Hidden Driver of Excellence*, celebrated author Daniel Goleman speaks to the importance of creating and sustaining focus in our endeavors:

> Directing attention toward where it needs to go is a primal task of leadership. Talent here lies in the ability to shift attention to the right place at the right time, sensing trends and emerging realities and seizing opportunities. But it's not just the focus of a single strategic decision-maker that makes or breaks a company: it's the entire array of attention bandwidth and dexterity among everyone in your organization.

A leader's field of attention—that is, the particular issues and goals s/he focuses on—guides the attention of those who follow her or him, whether or not the leader explicitly articulates it. People make their choices about where to focus based on their perception of what matters to leaders. The ripple effect gives leaders an extra load of responsibility: they are guiding not just their own attention but, to a large extent, *everyone else's*.

The point here is that the more you focus, the more your staff and colleagues will also seek to focus. And to quote Steve Jobs[10], "Deciding what **not** to do is as important as deciding what **to** do."

In this chapter, we've talked about prioritizing as a way to focus your decision-making, and to allow yourself to do a thoughtful review of the current decisions you and your team make. In the next chapter, we will jump into the most important part of the Decision Clarity practice—self-advocacy. With this next skill, you'll learn how to unleash the decision-making capacity of your organization. Self-advocacy is the backbone of the entire practice, and it builds on the skills of inventorying and prioritizing you've just completed.

Let us end with a cautionary tale. Some time ago, we met with a board member of a California nonprofit. This person revealed to us that he and his colleagues had recently fired their executive director. "What was her offense?" we asked. "She wanted to make all the decisions," he said. "She felt compelled to decide everything and we didn't find this to be an effective governance model. She made all the decisions ... until regrettably, she made none."

If, as an executive director, you can't prioritize, you'll either drive yourself and others crazy, or you'll work yourself out of a job. If, as a senior leader, you can't prioritize, you too will suffer inefficiency and ineffectiveness. If, as a staff member, you can't prioritize and advocate, you will risk squandering your talent and not contributing to your fullest. As such, in the next chapter, we'll show you and others in your ecosystem how to advocate for the decisions that will make the greatest difference to your organization and mission.

---

[10] "The Real Leadership Lessons of Steve Jobs." *Harvard Business Review*, April 2012.

KEY TAKEAWAYS

Determining which decisions you should *refrain* from making is just as important as determining which decisions *to* make.

Leaders who are making too many maintenance decisions aren't focusing on the key decisions that need their attention and are robbing staff of the opportunity to develop their decision-making abilities.

By prioritizing high-impact decisions, nonprofit leaders gain focus on those decisions that will move their organizations forward.

Not all decisions are created equally: some are "high impact" that will shape the future of organizations, and others are "maintenance" decisions that are less crucial.

Our ability to make decisions erodes as the day goes on, and the more we feel we have to make, the more drained we become; as such, it's vital to know how to prioritize.

The more you prioritize, the more your staff and colleagues will also seek to prioritize!

9

STEP THREE:
SELF-ADVOCACY

E very day, you walk up to a machine of some type and push its power button. Whether it's a copier, a computer, or a coffee machine, you touch a button to start the device. If only it were that easy to find our own source of power and access it without too much thought or ceremony. Imagine what would happen in our lives and organizations if we could simply "boot-up" our most forthright and yet compas-  sionate language, and say what we wanted to without fear or worry of retribution.

But pause a minute to consider that there are *already* places in our lives where we actually do this. We speak to what we want and wield our power quite naturally—and we do it almost without thinking. Take the Subway® sandwich shop, for example. If you've never frequented Subway, the process is simple. You walk up to the station and tell your designated sandwich maker what you want. You say, "I'd like a _____ on ___ with _____ and ____. I don't want ____ or _____. Thanks."

There's no pressure and you feel in control. You're not shrill or demanding; you're not afraid. You don't hesitate to give your order out of fear of rejection. You simply describe what you want, politely and respectfully. And if the store happens to be out of a particular item, the world doesn't come to an end—you merely specify your next preference. Why? Because you have the *language* you need to self-advocate, and you believe you have the *right* to say what you want.

This is what "self-advocacy" is. It is exactly what you do at a restaurant like Subway when ordering food, and it's the next step in the Decision Clarity process. Once you have inventoried your decisions and prioritized them, it's time to advocate by simply stating the role you want to play in each important decision, and why it makes sense. Believing you have the right to speak, you know that the person listening can say either "yes" or "no."

Sound simple? It *is* simple. Or at least the language is. But people in nonprofits often get tripped up when they must clearly state a want. Why? Because doing so is an act of belief and an act of power. And power, as we've discussed, often evokes fear.

UH-OH, HERE COMES FEAR AGAIN

In earlier chapters, we spoke about the three fears that are resident in nonprofits: fear of failure, fear of conflict, and fear of rejection. We've already talked about fear of failure and fear of conflict in detail. But it's the final fear, fear of rejection, that rears its head when people contemplate advocating for what they want.

For almost every person, the need to align and identify with an organization and peer group is a powerful force. We all want to belong. And that desire is so strong that some individuals stay quiet; they hesitate to state what they want for fear of being ostracized, even though actively communicating would benefit their organization and make their own lives more fulfilled.

In our work with nonprofits, we often see staff looking to their executive director to secure permission before they self-advocate. This is not unusual. In all work settings, employees will check to make sure that their actions are in accordance (or at least not directly in conflict) with the views of their managers. Nonprofits can be a little different, however, because of a fierce need to be part of a group. In this environment, when you start thinking about the act of stating what you want, you may come up against your own fear of rejection and conflict.

But these fears don't have to be show-stoppers. As we walk you through the process, we'll show you how advocating for the decision-making roles you want is completely doable—and will get easier over time. What's more, it can have a dramatic ripple effect in your organization, because once you start advocating for yourself, you may feel the power to encourage your peers or the people who work for you to do the same. The process feeds on itself, generating a heightened degree of openness around decision-making.

True-or-False Quiz

Before we delve in to this influential practice, we need to dispense with some common misperceptions around what self-advocating is and isn't. To do this, answer true or false to the following short, three-question quiz:

1. Self-advocating is the same as delegating. T/F?

2. Most executive directors resist their staff advocating for what they want because they want to keep their power. T/F?

3. If you tell people they have the power to self-advocate, they will run amok and damage their organization. T/F?

Answers

1. Self-advocating is the same as delegating. FALSE

Self-advocating is *not* delegating. Delegation is the process of being given power by a superior, and in that framework, the "power" you're given may or may not be what you *want*. You don't necessarily have a choice to accept delegation, because the decision or task is given to you by someone who has more influence. You can refuse to accept the assignment, but this may upset the balance of power between you and the person who is delegating. You can also be *asked* to be delegated to, but again, you're put in the position of asking someone above you in rank to *allow* you to exercise your own decision-making power.

Self-advocacy, in contrast, is about refocusing decision-making responsibility to advance the needs of the organization. When you self-advocate for the role you want in a particular decision, you're getting one step closer to exercising your own power and freeing yourself from externally—or internally—imposed limitations. You aren't waiting for someone more influential to gift you with power, and you aren't put in the position of having to accept something you don't want. Self-advocacy enables you to speak the truth about the decisions you want to make or contribute to. As such, it creates a more level playing field, where those who currently have power and those who have less agree to focus *together* on what's best and smartest for the organization's mission.

2. Most executive directors resist their staff advocating for what they want because they want to keep their power. FALSE.

While some nonprofit executive directors cling to power and decision-making out of ego or fear, our work has shown that these individuals represent a minority of the executive director population. Most leaders welcome a clarification of power and a redistribution of decision-making because they quite simply have too much to do. They would be open to taking this step if they were clear on who in their organization (or board) would be willing to stand up and take on the responsibility, with an understanding of who wants various roles on the support team (the Expert Advisor, the Contributor, the Informed, and/or the Driver).

3. If you tell people they have the power to self-advocate, they will run amok and ultimately damage their organization. FALSE.

We've rarely seen people advocate for decision-making authority that goes beyond their title; in fact, most tend to advocate for the decisions they thought they would be making when they took their position. We have likewise seen very few examples of nonprofit staff who have blatantly and selfishly pushed their own agenda at the expense of their organization. What we see more regularly is the opposite—staff who are afraid to self-advocate, lest they cross any perceived boundary of self-interest. People actually need convincing that they can assert their power, not the reverse.

Decision Clarity first walks people through a process for self-advocating that ensures requests for decision-making involvement are backed up by a rationale. It also involves a discussion process for leadership to grant or not grant the request, so any kind of "running amok" cannot actually happen.

THE LANGUAGE OF SELF-ADVOCACY

As you already know how to self-advocate on issues that involve your needs (such as ordering a meal), you're likely able to size up the options and to clearly state what you want (and what you're willing to do). In Decision Clarity, the language of self-advocacy is likewise straightforward. It follows a simple framework that states the decision being considered, the role you'd like to play, and your rationale.

Clear language is crucial to self-advocacy. If you can't be clear about what you want, chances are you won't get it. Moreover, imprecise language leads to confusion and misunderstandings. Here is an example of straightforward self-advocacy language:

"The _____ decision is important to my job and to our organization. I would like to advocate to serve in the role of _____."

Next, you will assert which role you'd like to play in the decision:

❖ **Decision-Maker** (I make the decision)

❖ **Expert Advisor** (I coach the person making the decision)

- ❖ **Contributor** (I meet with the Decision-Maker and contribute to their decision-making)

- ❖ **Informed** (I am informed of this decision sufficiently in advance so I can support the decision)

- ❖ **Driver** (I support the Decision-Maker by gathering information)

When doing this in a group context, you'll get immediate feedback from the leadership and members of your team, who may respond in a variety of ways:

- ❖ "I support you in that role."

- ❖ "I'm uncertain about you operating in that role; tell me more."

- ❖ "I don't support you in the role you're advocating for because _____."

- ❖ "Have you considered the role of_____ instead?"

Thank you for your support.

If you hear the "tell me more" response, you may have to give an explanation for why you want to take on this role. Have your rationale at the ready, but don't provide it unless you're asked for it. If you're new to self-advocating, the temptation is to defuse any anxiety you may be feeling by talking too much. Don't succumb to your own nervousness. Advocate for the role you want and be silent, without feeling compelled to fill up the space with your explanation.

If you're asked for an explanation, provide it, but make it simple. Succinctly say why you're the best person to take on this role, and show how doing so will advance the interests of your organization. Offer three to four sentences and then pause, waiting for the person to respond.

❖ If you get "I'll support you," congratulations! You've successfully self-advocated.

❖ If you get "I'm uncertain," ask what the concerns may be in a calm and direct manner, without being defensive.

❖ If you get "I don't support you," calmly ask why, listen carefully, respond if appropriate, and if the discussion can't go any further, reaffirm your interest in making or contributing to this decision in the future.

A Word on Tone

Having a calm and positive tone is important when self-advocating. Think back to the Subway example and recall that there's no concern or nervousness when ordering your sandwich. Assume you have every right to self-advocate, and you don't need to "get big" or "get small" in order to get what you want. The more you hesitate, or dance around the interaction, the less powerful you will feel.

And remember that you have talent, ideas, abilities, *and* power. If you express yourself clearly and calmly and it doesn't get you what you want, you haven't lost any influence; in fact, the bravery you've displayed has only made you more powerful. No matter what happens, you can make the interaction a good one for yourself by being direct in your communication and compassionate in your listening. If you don't attain your intended result, don't get flustered. Simply move on to another opportunity to self-advocate.

Why Self-Advocacy Makes a Positive Difference

Nonprofit organizations secure four high-level benefits when they create an environment where people can advocate for decision-making:

1. People are more willing to recognize and speak to decision-making bottlenecks and confusion.

2. People are more able to use their decision-making talents.

3. People become more focused on the key decisions that will make a difference.

4. The organization develops more capable Decision-Makers.

We urge self-advocacy because it frees people from externally imposed organizational processes and assumptions, and it allows nonprofits to make better use of their human capital by engaging the full complement of decision-makers (and decision-making teams) in their organization.

From a personal perspective, self-advocacy confers a sense of capability and well-being on those who can do it. People tell us all the time that they feel better about themselves and their jobs when they are able to exercise the kind of power they already feel is appropriate for their level.

WHAT TO EXPECT WHEN YOU SELF-ADVOCATE

Regardless of the position you hold in your organization, the act of self-advocating empowers you to speak the truth about the decisions you would like to make or contribute to. But just because you self-advocate does not mean you will always get what you want. As we have mentioned, there are checks and balances in the Decision Clarity system. The decisions you advocate for will still need to be approved by those who hold the final decision-making power in your organization.

In our work, we typically set expectations from the top down, using a process that looks like the following:

On the first day of our training, we ask the executive director or the most senior member of the staff to formally announce that s/he encourages all the members of the team to advocate to make (or contribute to) the decisions that affect their jobs. This person also says that s/he is open to realigning decision-making in the organization. While this person acknowledges having the final say in any decision-making changes, the commitment to openness is confirmed.

When an executive director brings us in, s/he is publicly acknowledging that there's either a problem or an opportunity to do even better. Either way, the person is expressing a willingness to make changes. This kind of public acknowledgement goes a long way. And the staff (or the board) is usually thrilled to take this opportunity to clarify the organization's decision-making. With everyone seeking to do things differently, there is pressure on multiple parts of the organization, and this pressure drives change.

In terms of acceptance/refusal rates, it's been our experience that executive directors and their leadership tend to accept most of the roles that are proposed to them. It is also worth noting that sometimes this process can shine a light on situations where people may not be suited for (or willing to take on) the responsibilities of a position.

In one of our engagements, for example, we interacted with a person who was struggling with the responsibilities of her job. Halfway through the engagement, she revealed to us that she was resigning her post. Through the Decision Clarity work, she gained the understanding to see that she did not want to continue in her job because she actually didn't want the responsibilities her position naturally required. She was relieved to discover this and was looking forward to letting the organization find someone who was better suited for the position, while she could be freed up to work in a position where she could shine.

Celebrated American author and humorist Mark Twain is quoted as saying, "Always do right. This will gratify some people and astonish the rest." As a nod to Mr. Twain, always advocate for the power and decision-making that will advance the mission of your organization. It will gratify some people and will astonish the rest—who will then find their voice and join you.

SELF-ADVOCACY ACTIVITIES

The following activities are designed to start you thinking about your own self-advocacy. These are preparation activities only—they will get you ready to fill out your Decision Clarity grids in the next chapter. Use the forms to write out your answers.

Activity 1:

What are the decisions you want to make?
Why are these the right decisions for you to advocate for?

Reflect on your prioritized list of decisions from Activity 5 in Chapter 8 (pp. 167–68). You should have three high-impact decisions you want to make, three you want to re-assign to others, three you want to take responsibility for, and three you want clarity on.

In the form below, list the three decisions you want to make and add any others that have come to mind that you deem appropriate. Then list the reasons you are the best person to make these decisions.

Decisions I Want to Advocate For	Reasons
1. I want to advocate to make the decision to:	
2. I want to advocate to make the decision to:	
3. I want to advocate to make the decision to:	

4. I want to advocate to make the decision to:	
5. I want to advocate to make the decision to:	
6. I want to advocate to make the decision to:	
7. I want to advocate to make the decision to:	

Activity 2:

What are the decisions you want to contribute to?

Why are these the right decisions for you?

Once again, look at your prioritized list of decisions from Activity 5 in Chapter 8 (pp. 167–68). You'll note that what's *missing* from this list are the decisions you want to contribute to. Think about this for a moment. What are the decisions where your input could be vital, even if you aren't the Decision-Maker? Where can you help as a Contributor?

In the form on the next page, list up to seven decisions you want to contribute to and *how* you want to contribute to these decisions.

Decisions I Want to Advocate to Contribute to	How I Want to Contribute
1. I want to contribute to the decision to:	
2. I want to contribute to the decision to:	
3. I want to contribute to the decision to:	
4. I want to contribute to the decision to:	
5. I want to contribute to the decision to:	
6. I want to contribute to the decision to:	
7. I want to contribute to the decision to:	

Activity 3:

What are the decisions you currently make that
you'd like to give up?

Why do you want to give up these decisions?

Using your prioritized list of decisions from Activity 5 in Chapter 8 (pp. 167–68), list the three decisions in the form below that you want to give to others. Add any others you deem appropriate, then list the reasons.

Decisions I Want to Assign to Others or Eliminate	Reasons
1. I want to eliminate the following decision from my responsibilities:	
2. I want to eliminate the following decision from my responsibilities:	
3. I want to eliminate the following decision from my responsibilities:	

4. I want to eliminate the following decision from my responsibilities:	
5. I want to eliminate the following decision from my responsibilities:	
6. I want to eliminate the following decision from my responsibilities:	
7. I want to eliminate the following decision from my responsibilities:	

SELF-ADVOCACY VS. BEING ASSIGNED

You don't need anyone's permission to self-advocate. The ability to speak your mind and express your desires is an inherent human right. You already know what decisions you are best equipped to make or contribute to, and by self-advocating you can create a clear path to the decisions that support your organization as a whole.

But the process of self-advocacy does not confer a "right" to make a particular set of decisions. Yes, you have the "right" to self-advocate, but you don't have a "right" to make a particular decision. In a 2005 article[11], Harvard Business School Professor Michael Jensen is quoted as saying that "allocating decision rights in ways that maximize organizational performance is an extraordinarily difficult and controversial management task."

Professor Jensen makes a vital point. *Assigning* decision rights is a perilous undertaking. Why? Just because someone has the most relevant information or experience doesn't mean this person is *best-equipped* or sufficiently *motivated* to make the decision for which s/he has been selected. Each individual's motivation and desire to make the decision needs to be taken into account when assigning decision-making authority.

Self-advocacy flips that challenge on its head. Leaders don't have to worry whether they're giving the right decisions to the right people. Leaders simply have to open a dialogue with their staff and create a space for self-advocacy. When each of us feels we have the power and the permission to advocate for the decisions we want, we move our organizations forward in ways that can ultimately benefit everyone.

SELF-ADVOCACY AS A POWER POSE

In her incredibly popular 2012 TED talk, "Your Body Language Shapes Who You Are," Harvard University Business School Professor and social scientist Amy Cuddy proposes the following question:

"... We know that our minds change our bodies; but is it also true that our bodies change our minds?"

She then asks:

"... what do the minds of the powerful versus the powerless look like?"

---

[11] Jacobs, Peter. "Decision Rights: Who Gives the Green Light?" *Harvard Management Update*, August, 2005.

Cuddy's research illustrates the physiological differences between those who have power and those who do not. Her work with primates shows that power in monkeys that are alpha (dominant) and non-alpha (non-dominant) can be measured physiologically with two hormones. Testosterone is the dominance hormone, and cortisol is the stress hormone. The alpha monkeys show high testosterone and low cortisol; the non-alpha monkeys show lower testosterone and higher cortisol. She summarizes by saying:

"So what does this mean? When you think about power, people tend to think about testosterone because that's about dominance. But really, power is also about how you react to stress."

What's interesting about Cuddy's work is she has found that physiology is *not* static; power isn't something "we're born with." When an alpha monkey suddenly gets knocked out and a new non-alpha monkey needs to take over, within a few days, the new monkey's testosterone goes up significantly and its cortisol drops significantly. Power can be measured physiologically, but it is also influenced by outside circumstances.

Cuddy goes on to explain how something she calls "power poses" can actually change the mind's physiology and enable a person to feel more powerful. A power pose looks like this:

Dr. Cuddy asserts that if you do this pose for two minutes a day, you will feel more powerful—she has tested this in her lab and the results are significant. If we act more powerful, we feel more powerful, and then we become more powerful. We change our power chemistry by changing our minds, and we change our minds by changing our bodies.

Put another way, our feelings of powerlessness get in the way of what we think we can do. As we discussed in prior chapters, your views on power and decision-making are shaped by your gender, race, age, class, sexual orientation, personal psychology, and more. And all of us have pain around power, which we have come by through our experience. Even those who have power are not without their pain and fear.

Self-advocacy is the part of Decision Clarity that engenders the most fear in participants —but it also generates the most excitement. It is informed by the belief that if we create the opportunity for members of the organization to advocate without fear or recrimination, they will reveal the most effective decision-making distribution for their organization. People already know how things should work; the Decision Clarity practice provides the structure and permission that encourages this to emerge.

Self-advocacy is the power pose of Decision Clarity. The process itself allows you to feel more influential. As you put your fear and uncertainty aside, you champion the decisions you want to make or be involved in. And the more you advocate for yourself, the more comfortable you will be—and the more powerful you'll become.

KEY TAKEAWAYS

When people self-advocate, they usually succeed.

Human beings engage in self-advocacy every day, but we hesitate to do so when the power and decision-making rules are unclear, or when we fear for our position.

In order to successfully create a culture of self-advocacy, everyone engaged in the Decision Clarity process must use the same self-advocacy language:

"The _____ decision is important to my job and to our organization. I would like the opportunity to serve in the role of _____."

Self-advocacy is *not* delegation. Delegation is achieved when someone with more power gives a decision to someone with less power, whereas the language of self-advocacy enables people to advocate for the specific decisions they want to make or support.

Engaging in self-advocacy does not guarantee that you will be awarded the decision-making that you seek, but don't let that dissuade you—not every decision may be right for you at a given time.

Self-advocacy increases accountability and erases ambiguity.

Self-advocacy creates true empowerment, allowing people to be better equipped to tackle the decisions for which they have advocated. Even if they aren't awarded a particular decision, they feel better for having the courage to speak up.

CREATING DECISION CLARITY GRIDS

Here's a sign I once encountered:

(In golf, "carry" is the distance the ball travels through the air.)

This sign doesn't mince words—"Aim here and unleash the power in you." It reminds the reader that even though the goal seems far away, if you aim for it and take a mighty swing, you will defy any inner doubts you have and land where you want to be. It encourages you to put away any fears you have and dare to be bold. Rather than chipping your way down the course, why not send the ball flying?

This is the same attitude you need when constructing Decision Clarity grids. We've talked a lot about power and the fears associated with it. This next-to-final step is another concrete action that helps you face these unspoken dynamics and transform them into something constructive.

This chapter builds on the first three skills you've already mastered (inventorying, prioritizing, and advocating), and now culminates with filling out a grid that illuminates the important decisions you want to advocate for and the key roles you want. This step marries your thinking about decisions with your ideas about which people in your organization are best suited to be the Decision-Maker, Expert Advisor, Contributor, Informed, and/or Driver, as well as the planned completion date for each decision. Once you complete your grid, you'll then have the opportunity to talk about its contents in person, and advocate for specific decisions and roles.

The grid you will create in this chapter is your stake in the ground and the main product of the Decision Clarity practice. Once people see what you've advocated for, this simple but powerful act will allow you to engage in conversations that might otherwise be too difficult to manage. Creating your Decision Clarity grid is easy, yet it carries the benefit of changing the decision-making environment in your nonprofit in concrete and positive ways.

SAMPLE DECISION CLARITY GRIDS

The grid on the following two pages is a sample that highlights the important decisions facing a particular team member, as well as her ideas about which decisions she wants to take full responsibility for, and who will be the members of her decision-making team. Note: In this grid, the author is appointed as the Decision-Maker for most of the decisions, but advocates for others to be the Decision-Maker as well.

As you look at the examples, note how specific the language is for each decision— each begins with the word "decide." We do this on purpose to bring each decision that's being advocated for into clear focus.

DECISION CLARITY GRID #1

Decision to Be Made	Decision-Maker	Expert Advisor(s)	Contributor	Informed	Driver	Comp Date
Financials: Decide who we use as our book-keepers	Chris Shay	Steven Truong	Steve Greenberg	Marge Fuller	Augustine Barber	4/22/15
Decide on our bookkeeping process	Chris Shay	Victor Chu	Alice Kuo	Steph Caradine		4/22/15
Decide where we store financial information	Chris Shay	Victor Chu	Babs Hanson	Steven Truong		4/22/15
Decide how we invoice and track A/R	Chris Shay	Alice Kuo	Glenn Birtz	Saira Abdullah		4/22/15
Decide how expenses are reported and tracked	Chris Shay	Steven Truong	Steve Greenberg	Steph Caradine		4/22/15
Decide how income is reported and tracked	Chris Shay	Steven Truong	Alice Kuo	Marge Fuller	Augustine Barber	4/22/15
HR: Decide how job descriptions are created and revised	Chris Shay	Tomas Jimenez	Babs Hanson	Marge Fuller		5/29/15
Decide what benefits we offer employees	Chris Shay	Steven Truong	Babs Hanson	Steph Caradine		5/29/15
Decide on the on-boarding and off-boarding process for new hires	Chris Shay	Tomas Jimenez	Alice Kuo	Steph Caradine		5/29/15
Office Management: Decide when/where board meetings are	Chris Shay	Steven Truong	Steve Greenberg	Marge Fuller		6/15/15
Development: Decide our thank-you process for donations	Chris Shay	Saira Abdulla, Julie Abrams	Babs Hanson	Steven Truong	Elliah Stoneback	4/15/15

Decision to Be Made	Decision-Maker	Expert Advisor(s)	Contributor	Informed	Driver	Comp Date
Program: Decide where to store program kits and materials	Alice Kuo	Chris Shay	Tomas Jimenez	Steph Caradine		6/12/15
Decide how much inventory to keep on hand	Alice Kuo	Tomas Jimenez	Steve Greenberg	Chris Shay		6/12/15
Decide what conferences the program team attends	Neeru Chopra	Ellen Rye	Babs Hanson	Chris Shay		6/12/15

Here is another example. Note that this grid is similar to the first, but the person who completed it has a different role, and therefore different high-impact decisions to consider.

DECISION CLARITY GRID #2

Decision to Be Made	Decision-Maker	Expert Advisor	Contributor	Informed	Driver	Comp Date
Decide on the goals of the strategic plan	Steven Truong	Elaine Levy	April Kzyanski			6/8/15
Decide on the development goal	Steven Truong	Pat Singer	Tomas Jimenez, Carlos Ramirez			6/8/15
Decide what insurance we should purchase	Chris Shay	Steven Truong	Tomas Jimenez			5/29/15
Decide how our video should be revised	Leslie Jackson	Al Tomak	Saul Stanley	Steven Truong		6/15/15
Decide on our board recruitment strategy	Steven Truong	Stephen Silver	Board			6/15/15

Decision to Be Made	Decision-Maker	Expert Advisor	Contributor	Informed	Driver	Comp Date
Decide on our marketing goals	Carlos Ramirez	Steven Truong	Saira Abdullah		Augustin Barber	6/15/15
Decide on our development prospects	Steven Truong	Julie Petrides	Saira Abdullah			6/15/15
Decide how to follow up with event participants	Saira Abdullah	Steven Truong	Carlos Ramirez	Chris Shay		6/15/15
Decide who should manage our camps	Tomas Jimenez	Steven Truong	Leslie Jackson	Saira Abdullah		6/15/15

Each of these sample grids specifies a person in a role for each decision. To refresh your memory, here is a quick review of the roles:

1. Decision-Maker

The person who advocates for making a particular decision. The Decision-Maker is not a recommender or an information-gatherer; rather s/he is the person who has or will be entrusted with the responsibility for making the actual decision.

2. Expert Advisor

The person who coaches the Decision-Maker to make the best decision, consulting with the Decision-Maker to provide guidance as needed. As a last resort, the advisor can also bring concerns to the executive director, if s/he is worried about the Decision-Maker's focus or abilities. There should be no more than one or two advisors per decision.

3. Contributor

The person who has knowledge of one or more aspects of the decision, and would like to share advice, thoughts, or concerns with the Decision-Maker. Contributors are people who should have a say in a particular decision, but are often overlooked.

4. Informed

These people play a role in the execution of the decision, and need to be kept abreast on a timely basis so they can bring their efforts to bear on the decision. They aren't the people who merely receive the announcement email at the end, but rather those who need to be aware of what is happening because it may affect the decision (and their own work) in the more immediate term.

5. Driver

This optional role is used when the Decision-Maker needs additional information gathering, organizational assistance, or analytical assistance. Depending on the complexity of the decision, you may need more than one driver. Only 10–20% we've vetted have required this role.

As you see, the Decision Clarity grid offers a structure for you to lay out all the important decisions that lie ahead of you, with places for you to name who will play which role in each decision. Once you have your list compiled and roles assigned, you then get to advocate for the roles on your grid. Creating a grid and then advocating for its contents are two actions that go together. But first, let's focus on what you need to know to create your grid.

FOUR STEPS TO FILLING OUT YOUR DECISION CLARITY GRID

Before you fill out your grid, ask yourself the following four questions:

1. Do I understand my organization's strategic plan or key objectives?

2. Which high-impact decisions affect my job?

3. What role, if any, do I want to play in these decisions?

4. Who should be on my unified decision-making team?

Understand Your Organization's Strategic Plan or Key Objectives

If you don't already have a solid understanding of your organization's strategic plan or key objectives, you need to acquire one. The components of the strategic plan drive the decisions you need to make, so you must be grounded in the major objectives that your organization seeks to achieve. Without this grounding, you may be working on decisions that are inconsequential. You want to make sure that what you're focused on is aligned with where the organization is heading.

If your organization has a strategic plan, make sure you read it. If you don't have a strategic plan, procure the document that best identifies what the organization (or your department within the organization) is trying to achieve. If you have a manager, talk with this person, and make sure you're certain of the major objectives s/he wants you to accomplish. Armed with knowledge of your strategic plan and a working understanding of our model, you'll be able to answer the questions below.

Which High-Impact Decisions Affect My Job?

Take a look at the activities you completed in Chapters 7–9. These will give you a baseline for where to begin.

Grid-Creating Activity 1:

Comprehensive Inventory

Use the language below, and list the decisions that most affect your job.

"The decision to _____ affects my job and I want a role in its resolution."

As with the other inventories you've created, try not to censor yourself; simply write a list without stopping until you've exhausted all the obvious high-impact decisions in your position and area of expertise. This is the time to set your sights broad, and make as long a list as you can. If you feel that you're censoring yourself or injecting shame or fear into your analysis, try to resist those temptations by prioritizing honesty. You can use the form below.

DECISION CLARITY GRID (INVENTORY)

These high-impact decisions affect my job, and I want a role in their resolution:
1.
2.
3.
4.
5.
6.
7.
8.

| 9. |
| 10. |
| 11. |
| 12. |
| 13. |
| 14. |
| 15. |

Once you've completed your list, consider the following questions:

❖ Is your list longer or shorter than you would have imagined?

❖ Did you come up with new decisions you had not previously been aware of or considered?

❖ Do you feel overwhelmed looking at the decisions on your list, or do you feel empowered because you have them all down on paper?

❖ Does the list lessen any anxiety you may have had and give you a stronger sense of certainty about the decisions that affect your job?

Next, verify that this list is an accurate representation of all the high-impact decisions that affect your job. Have you forgotten anything? If you discover you have, add it in. Don't be constrained by the size of the form.

Once you have a complete list, make sure that each decision is indeed one you want to play a role in resolving.

❖ If you're hesitant to play a role in a decision that affects your job, take a moment to consider why this is so. Perhaps your focus is elsewhere, or maybe the decision represents a matter that is too sensitive for you.

❖ If the decision isn't one you want to be directly involved in, keep it on your list anyway. If you don't want to take responsibility for it, part of the benefit of writing it down is to set the stage to make sure someone else does.

Grid-Creating Activity 2:
Prioritizing the Inventory

You may have already guessed that the next thing to do is organize and prioritize your inventory. Take a moment to put your decisions into categories (if you find categories helpful). Reorganize your list so that the most important decisions are at the top of the list. Consult the sample grids if you need ideas.

DECISION CLARITY GRID (PRIORITIZATION)

These high-impact decisions affect my job, and I want a role in their resolution:
1.
2.
3.
4.
5.
6.
7.
8.
9.
10.

Once you have an organized, prioritized inventory, you're ready for the next step—one we've talked a lot about but haven't yet practiced: advocating for roles.

What Role Do I Want to Play in These Decisions?

Now, look at the decisions in your inventory and consider the following questions: On which decisions do I want to be the:

Decision-Maker?

(Person entrusted with the responsibility for making the decision)

Expert Advisor?

(Person who coaches the Decision-Maker to make the best decision)

Contributor?

(Person who has knowledge, and would like to share advice, concern, or thoughts with the Decision-Maker)

Informed?

(Person who needs to be informed in order to play a role in the execution of the decision)

Driver?

(Person who can support the Decision-Maker in gathering information, talking to people, and doing preliminary analysis)

Decision-maker Expert/Advisor Contributor Informed Driver

> If you're a member of the organization, you can look at roles that affect you and other people on your team or in your department. If you're a board member, you can use your grid to delineate the decisions that you believe should belong to the board and those that should fall to your executive director.

Grid-Creating Activity 3:

Assigning Roles

Using your prioritized inventory from the activity you've just completed and the roles you've determined are best for you, fill in the grid on the next page with your first and last name (not your title). It's been our experience that explicitly putting first and last names on your grid yields better results than using titles, which put less "skin in the game" for those who advocate. There's nothing like seeing your name on a grid to spur action.

Remember, you don't always have to be the Decision-Maker. It's often wise to claim decision-making for those that are most important to you, and to take support roles for decisions that are less crucial. For example, perhaps you could mentor an up-and-coming manager by serving as his or her Expert Advisor.

Some of the decisions on your list may affect your job, but compared to other key decisions in your arena, they might better be given to others—allowing you to take a Contributor or even an Informed role. Think through the best mix of roles for you, approaching the activity with an open mind, and being aware of any tendencies you have to take on responsibility that might be unhelpful to you in the long run.

DECISION CLARITY GRID

Decision to Be Made	Decision-Maker	Expert Advisor	Contributor	Informed	Driver	Comp Date

To obtain a downloadable version of the Decision Clarity Grid,
visit www.scheiergroup.com/tools.

Grid-Creating Activity 4:

Double-Check

Take a moment to review your grid and ensure you have all the information you need. While it's important to unleash the power in you, it's always best to advocate from a position of strength and insight.

1. First, do a decision-check:

   ❖ Is the decision clearly framed?

   ❖ Are you clear about its importance to the organization?

   ❖ If you need additional information, ask for it.

   ❖ If you're advocating for another role, consider how you will support the Decision-Maker and if you need any special information to facilitate this strategy.

2. Second, do a rationale-check:

   ❖ Do you have a rationale that—if necessary—you can share with your colleagues for why you are best-suited to serve in the roles you have advocated for, and how your participation in this decision will advance your mission?

Advocating is an act of confidence that is best based on the conviction that the decisions and the roles you are seeking will benefit your organization if they are granted. Remember, you are speaking up to move your organization forward, not just to advance your own interests. While you can do both, you don't want to be perceived as acting solely out of self-interest. How do you guard against that perception? By making sure in your own mind that you possess a rationale for why you're best suited to take on these responsibilities.

It's crucial in this process not to be shy. You may have talents, skills, and experiences that no one in your organization knows you possess; as such, you may be the perfect person to make or contribute to decisions for which others wouldn't have thought of you. Stick to your instincts, develop your rationale, and get ready to advocate. Most people champion decisions commonly associated with their roles, but even decisions people have been afraid to take on (or were unsure they could) are usually affirmed. And while people are rarely questioned about the roles for which they have asserted, we'll talk in the next chapter about how to deal with this situation if it arises.

WHO SHOULD BE ON MY UNIFIED DECISION-MAKING TEAM?

Now that you have thought carefully about advocating for the roles you would like to play in making the decisions on your list, you need to fill out the rest of your grid. Looking at the decisions on the left-hand side on the grid, ask yourself: Who else should have a stake in the decisions I've listed?

Grid-Creating Activity 5:

Assigning Your Team

Take a look at the ecosystem chart you created in Chapter 3 (p. 68) and write down the names of the people who will be affected by the decisions you make. These people will comprise your initial list of Contributors in each category. It's important to list them so you have a complete sense of the human capital resources you can utilize.

First, let's look at who will be the Expert Advisor for each decision before you. You may not believe you need someone in this role, or worry that your organization is so small that involving someone as an Expert Advisor would tax your organization too much, but we encourage you to reject both of these notions.

The Expert Advisor exists to provide counsel to the Decision-Maker, functioning as a coach and resource. While this person has *no* decision-making responsibility, s/he provides support and some measure of oversight. For example, if your Expert Advisor believes that you, as the Decision-Maker, are headed down the wrong path, s/he should give this counsel. Likewise, if your Expert Advisor doesn't think specific elements are handled appropriately, s/he may elect to take this concern to the executive director, being judicious as to how many times this happens. The focus of this role is to support you in a way that affirms trust and doesn't limit your creativity or initiative.

Think about the two or three people who can best serve as Expert Advisors for you in your role as Decision-Maker. Then, ask yourself:

❖ Whom do you trust most?

❖ Who will push you to make a better decision?

❖ Who knows a great deal about the issues that have to be weighed when you make your decision?

These are the attributes you want in your Expert Advisor: trust, honesty, and knowledge. If this person possesses these three attributes, you have the right person. For each decision on your list, be sure to have at least one—but not more than two—Expert Advisors. You may be forced to balance advice, and doing this with more than two people is a recipe for confusion. Once you've determined who would make the best Expert Advisor(s) for each decision before you, write their first and last name(s) (not their titles) on your grid.

Now, for each decision on your list, consider who is best equipped to play a role as a Contributor in your decision-making efforts. Remember, these are people who have relevant knowledge and would like to share advice, concern, or thoughts with the Decision-Maker. Write down the first and last names of these people, noting that it's not unusual to list as many as five or more people as Contributors for each decision.

Now let's move on to those who need to be Informed. These are the team members who need information so they can take an active role in implementing or promoting your decision. As we've discussed, these are not the people who merely receive the announcement email and have no real stake in the outcome; rather, they have a stake, but aren't interested in being the Decision-Maker, Expert Advisor, or Contributor. They have a vested interest because they either have to put time into implementing your decision, or your decision will affect their jobs.

Why is it important to list those who need to be informed? Because we've all been in situations where someone has made a decision without advising us of it in a timely fashion. How many perfectly good weekends have been ruined in this way? If you're unaware of the decisions that will affect you, how can you prepare to execute on the results of them?

Now, add to your grid the first and last names of all the people who have good reason to be informed of your decision, both before and after you make it. It's not unusual to have as many as three or more in this category.

Last, the Driver is an optional role in the Decision Clarity practice. If the decision before you is so large that you require the assistance of someone to gather data, talk with stakeholders, or generally support you, then a Driver is also needed. Again, only 10–20% of the Decision-Makers who use our grids make use of the Driver role. If the decision before you requires such a role, consider which person in your organization is best suited to serve in this way.

Keep in mind that this role often goes to an entry-level staff person who is willing to work under the direction of the Decision-Maker. It can also go to someone the Decision-Maker would like to groom to take on more responsibility. As you consider this person, ask yourself:

❖ Who has the most appropriate skills?

❖ Who has the most determination?

❖ Who will have the courage?

Write down this person's first and last name on your grid for each decision that merits this role, along with the date by which you want the decision to be made. The addition of the date makes the decision-making responsibility concrete.

Congratulations! You've now completed your initial Decision Clarity grid! While you have created this first version on your own, the real benefit comes from interacting with your colleagues and management to champion what's on your grid. Advocating for yourself and encouraging others to do the same will be a powerful accelerant for your organization, and in Chapter 11, we'll provide strategies for engaging your colleagues in the transformation.

THE POWER OF LANGUAGE

By adopting the Decision Clarity practice, you have not only acquired a philosophy around decision-making and organized and clarified your thoughts, but you have become proficient in the Decision Clarity *language*. This language will allow you to feel comfortable discussing power and decision-making, enabling you to say:

"I'm advocating to be the Decision-Maker for the _____ decision." OR

"I'm advocating to be the Expert Advisor for the _____ decision." OR

"I'm advocating to be a Contributor for the _____ decision." OR

"I'm advocating to be Informed (on a timely basis) about the _____ decision so I can do my part to make sure it comes out right." OR

"I'm advocating to be the Driver for the _____ decision to help the Decision-Maker gather the information s/he needs."

When you implement this practice within a group, individuals will use this language and their colleagues will know what they mean. Everyone will feel relieved that they can talk about power and decision-making without feeling awkward—no one will be offended, and everyone will understand they have permission to advocate for a particular role for each decision that affects their job. Being this transparent eliminates confusion, reduces conflict, and increases decision-making focus. Best of all, you can lead by example.

The D-E-C-I-D roles are not just categories—they combine to create unified decision-making teams for each decision you enter into the process. These roles provide certainty about your behavior and the behavior of others. If you have a role, you operate in that role. If you have a change of heart about the role you want, you have to advocate for a revision.

The D-E-C-I-D roles create fair operating environments and trust. If you know what decisions are yours to make and you understand that you won't be overruled unless you're driving the train off the track, you'll have the courage to champion the decisions that are important to you.

Our work in nonprofits has shown us that a shared knowledge of the Decision Clarity practice and consistent use of the language creates a significant advantage for organizations. We've been pleased to see that years after our engagements have concluded, organizations that have maintained the same leadership continue to use the Decision Clarity language and method to clarify who will be making the high-impact decisions in their organization. The bottom line is: this practice works and has staying power.

FINAL GRID-CONSTRUCTION INSIGHTS

You now know how to fill out a Decision Clarity grid, but before we go on to the next chapter where you advocate for what's on your grid, we need to make one final point: Decision Clarity is a method for driving decisions down to the people who are best equipped to make them, but it does *not* inherently change the organizational structure of your nonprofit. While Decision Clarity focuses on clarifying your decision-making, your job, title, and responsibilities are still yours. If you're an executive director, you remain so; if you're on the board or staff, you maintain the same role.

By making your Decision Clarity grid, you haven't destroyed the organizational chart or altered the structure of your organization. What you *have* done is create an explicit way to talk about and divide decision-making and power. The time you dedicate to this task is invaluable, and it can change the course of your organization's development in truly incredible ways.

KEY TAKEAWAYS

Creating a Decision Clarity grid is an act of power that solidifies the decisions that each person is committed to working on.

Don't be afraid to list all the high-impact decisions that affect your job or to advocate to make the contribution that you want to make.

Before advocating to make or support a particular decision, participants need to understand their organization's strategic plan, identify which high-impact decisions in that plan affect their job, and determine what role they want to play in these decisions.

A shared knowledge of the Decision Clarity practice and consistent use of the language creates a significant advantage for organizations, one that has proven staying power.

Your grid will reflect all your decisions at hand, along with the relevant parties who should contribute to each.

STEP FOUR:
ENGAGING AND COMMUNICATING

We are nearing the home stretch! After completing your Decision Clarity grid, listing in detail each of the high-impact decisions affecting your job and documenting the assigned roles for yourself and the other members of your unified decision-making teams, the fog is hopefully dissipating, and the future ahead should be getting clearer.

Be proud of yourself as this is a big step forward. This is probably the first time you (and other members of your nonprofit) have generated such a visual, and when you share your grids, you will be able to see who is making which decisions across the entire spectrum of your work group, department, or even your entire organization.

ADVOCATING PUBLICLY AND GETTING FEEDBACK

The goal of this last step in the process is to share your grid publicly so that you and your team can all get on the same page. This is when you communicate your intentions to others, learn where your name surfaces on other grids, and receive feedback on any modifications you need to make.

All the people who are listed on your grid have an immediate stake in how you handle the decisions you've listed. And the leadership of your organization (whether they're listed on your grid or not) will also want to see what you've advocated for. This is why you have a meeting.

At this meeting, each person will have the opportunity to present his or her grid, using the language you've practiced in Chapter 9 to discuss and advocate for the decisions listed.

MANAGEMENT REVIEW

Before you arrive at the meeting, your team leader must review all the grids. If you are the team leader, gather the completed grids and review them prior to your feedback meeting. If you're not the team leader, encourage this person to review all grids and then call a feedback meeting.

If you are the person reviewing the grids, here are the questions to consider:

❖ How surprised are you by the number of decisions that people have listed on the grids before you?

❖ Are all the important decisions confronting your team, department, or organization represented across all the grids?

❖ Are the people most relevant to the decisions advocating for them? Are the people in support roles (Contributors, the Informed, and Drivers) the ones you think should be involved?

❖ Are the Expert Advisors the people who can dispense advice without interference? And do they have the right background and experience to be of value to the Decision-Maker?

Consider the integrity of each decision-making team, and whether you believe the team can adequately support the decision.

THE DETRIMENT OF IMPLICIT BIAS

When reviewing the grids, it's vital to be conscious of your biases. Everyone wants to believe that his or her views are unbiased and based on a specific set of incontrovertible facts, but sadly, this is not true. We all have biases and they often come into play in our decision-making. Some are explicit and benign—like our preferences for hiking spots, morning coffee, or meeting times. Others are hidden and potentially harmful—like our positive or negative mental attitude toward a person (or thing or group) that we hold on an unconscious level. Implicit biases can have an unwelcome effect on our decision-making if allowed to operate unchecked.

The cartoon below[12] is a perfect example of an implicit bias. The dogs in the meeting assume that the cat is up to no good; it's "natural logic" from the dogs' perspectives. But the question is, do the dogs in this cartoon seem to be open to what the cat might want to say? Not really. And what is the effect of that bias? The dog probably can't hear what the cat has to say, even if it's a perfectly appropriate idea or question.

"This had better be good."

Have you ever been in a meeting and felt like the cat?
Have you ever acted like the dog?

---

[12] Wood, Paul. *Harvard Business Review*, November 2013.

The point here is that implicit biases can have an unwelcome effect on your views on decision-making. When you review the grids, pay attention to the biases that start coming to the surface about the abilities and judgment of your staff. Are people advocating for decision-making or support roles that you think are surprising (or even alarming)? Are you uncertain about how wise it would be to give some of the people on your team certain roles? Just because you're working in a social-impact field doesn't mean you are without bias. Pay attention to these reactions, but make space for another perspective.

The Decision Clarity grids have been cited by many of our clients as an effective organizing and project management tool, but they've been noted as a valuable accountability tool as well. When people create their grids, they are making a public declaration about what they want to do. And once approved, people are invested with decision-making power and are responsible for the outcomes they create. There's nothing squishy about it. So keep in mind as you review the grids, that each author has taken a risk and put a lot on the line.

We all have biases. But as the leader of your team, group, or organization, your job in this stage of the process is to keep them in check. Yes, the grid author may have previously disappointed you. Perhaps you believe that s/he may not be experienced enough or have shown the maturity to make (or support) the decisions on her or his grid. Maybe the person advocating to make a decision didn't go to an elite school, or doesn't look or act or sound like you. But keep in mind that the grid author took the brave step to advocate for a role and a decision that is important to your organization. You want to recognize and cultivate this kind of initiative.

Ultimately, these people want to take on a bigger role in your organization, so unless you can make a specific argument like "You have too much to do to focus on X," or "You don't have the experience to do Y," our advice is to let the people on your team advocate for what they would like to do. If they are championing a responsibility, they will try hard not to let you down.

According to a recent Gallup study[13], engaged employees are people who "are involved in, enthusiastic about, and committed to their work, and contribute to their

---

[13] "The State of the American Workplace: Employee Engagement Insights for Business Leaders," 2013.

organization in a positive manner," while disengaged employees are those who "are emotionally disconnected from their workplaces and less likely to be productive." Disengaged employees are also "more likely to steal from their companies, negatively influence their coworkers, miss workdays, and drive customers or clients away."

This makes intuitive sense, and the study advances a number of strategies for encouraging employee engagement. One such strategy is to "focus on engagement at the enterprise and local level." According to the study, leaders accomplish this by "weaving employee engagement into performance expectations for managers (and staff), and enabling them to execute on those expectations. Managers and employees must feel empowered by leadership to make a significant difference in their immediate environment." Advocating is a key to engagement, and allowing managers and employees to champion roles and decisions they want to make and support is a great way to help them feel engaged.

If you can't in good faith endorse what a person on your team has advocated for, you *will* have the opportunity to speak up. Make note of your concerns or questions and be prepared to speak to them at the next stage of the process—the team meeting.

As we'll detail shortly, the grids before you are tools to monitor progress on decisions that are important to your organization. If the people responsible for making or supporting a decision aren't doing their job, you can always alter the arrangement at that time. Many leaders long to find themselves with an employee base that actually *wants* to take responsibility for the crucial decisions in their environment. Take a look at what people have advocated for, and do your best to support them.

THE GRID REVIEW MEETING

Once the grids have been reviewed, it's time to gather your colleagues to advocate in public and get feedback on your grids. In order to have a successful meeting, our experience indicates that there are four best practices.

Step 1:
Opening Reassurance

Advocating for decision-making power doesn't always come naturally, and many people are uncomfortable doing it the first time—especially in front of their colleagues and management. Sometimes people find it difficult to shake off their natural reticence and find themselves wanting to play it safe. When the meeting starts, it's important for the most senior person in the room to reaffirm that participants are free to advocate for making (or supporting) the decisions they each think are crucial to their jobs.

Even though it's a bit formal, we urge the senior person in the room to read the following statement:

"I (name) _____ (title) _____ at_____
(organization) do solemnly affirm that:

I want all members of this team to fully advocate for the decisions and the roles that are reflective of your talent and experience, and to offer innovative solutions to our decision-making challenges.

Please advocate without fear or worry of any negative consequence. All advocating will be treated respectfully, and there will be no penalties for advocating."

We call this the "Free and Fair Participation Guarantee," and it has had a notably positive affect on individual and group participation. If you're the senior person in the room reading this statement, it will set a positive tone for what's to come.

Step 2:
Setting the Rules

Now that the preliminary reassurance is out of the way, people will feel safer in presenting their grids. We suggest at this point that the meeting leader restate the purpose of the meeting (i.e., to present the individual grids and get feedback), and set expectations and rules.

As any lingering confusion or hesitation can bring out fear in the participants, it's crucial that this initial communication be clear and encouraging. People will still be looking to make sure their management intends to go through with this process, so if there is hesitation in the room, be mindful of this and carry on. People will watch what you do; if they doubt your words, they will make note of your actions. If your actions are consistent with this process, you will build the trust you need.

Here's a sample script for how the introduction might sound:

"Thank you for attending this meeting. As you know, we're here today to present our individual Decision Clarity grids and to receive feedback on this material. Just as I urged you all to advocate freely, let me also urge you to give feedback freely. Here's how I want today's session to go: We'll each take a turn reviewing the decisions on our grids and walking the group through the people we think are best able to assist us. But I (and the other managers) will go last. I want you to advocate without fear, and without being unduly influenced by my grid.

"The person presenting will review each decision on their grid. They'll state the decision they're advocating to make (or support) and then list the rest of the people on their unified decision-making team. If you're on this person's grid and want to be, say, "I'm good." If you're not on this person's grid and want to be, tell us what role you want. If you're on this person's grid and don't want to be, or want to be in a different role, speak up.

"If there's conflict as to who is on a particular grid that we can't resolve in the meeting, then the two people will meet with me and work it out. I doubt I'll have to do that, though. If we have to take a decision out of the group setting, I'll let you know what happens.

"Each person will have 15 minutes to review his/her grid with the group. Any questions?"

Here's a quick recap of the order of your meeting:

- Give each person 15 minutes to present his or her entire grid to the team. In this process, s/he states each decision s/he is advocating to make (or support), and then lists the rest of the people on the unified decision-making team.

- Each person advocates freely and receives feedback from his or her colleagues.

- Participants say, "I support this," if they are on someone's grid and satisfied with the assigned role. If a participant is not on someone's grid and wants to be, s/he tells the person and the group what role s/he wants to play. If a participant is on someone's grid and doesn't want to be (or wants a different role), s/he simply speaks up.

❖ If there's conflict that can't be resolved in the meeting (as to who is on a particular grid), then the two people meet with the leader and work it out (although follow-up meetings to resolve conflict are rare). If this meeting does happen, the leader must report the final results of the deliberations to the group.

❖ The leader presents her or his grid last, so as not to influence the grids of the less senior people on the team.

Step 3:
Advocating and Getting Feedback

Advocating for the decisions on each grid is quite straightforward. Remember the Subway sandwich example? Reviewing a grid is an action that is done as calmly as ordering a sandwich. Everything you need to know is on the grid, so there's no reason to be concerned, panic, or be defensive.

We recommend that participants take it one decision at a time, and be clear about the decision they are advocating to make (or support). They can read the names on the line and pause when done. At the end of each decision they ask, "Does anyone have any questions?"

Feedback generally comes in four ways:

1. **Support**:

    "I support you to make this decision and the role you've chosen."

2. **Need More Information:**

    "I'm uncertain about the decisions (or role) you're advocating for; please tell me more."

3. **Don't Support:**

    "I don't support you in the decision (or role) for which you have advocated because _____."

4. **Other Options:**

    "Have you considered this role instead?" Or "Is there another role you'd like to play (or have me play)?"

Team members discuss the grids and their concerns. If there is no concrete feedback, the participants go on and read the next decision. The point is to keep the meeting moving.

While it's important to keep on track, everyone needs to be prepared that people may indeed have questions, and they may want to advocate to add or to subtract someone from the grids. This is all normal, but what if during the discussion a decision on your grid is materially changed in a way that you now find untenable? What do you do? The answer is to simply advocate for removing the decision from your grid. If you don't want to take responsibility for this newly reformulated decision, then advocate for someone else to do so.

The goal of the process is for you to have a list of decisions and goals that you can unflinchingly embrace. If you can't fully adopt a decision and your role in it, then respectfully eliminate it from your grid.

Step 4:

Affirmation

The second-to-last step in the process may seem superfluous, but it is truly important to reinforce to participants that a major change has just occurred. Affirmation marks that a handoff has taken place, and that the advocating the participants have done has not been in vain.

If the manager is satisfied with the decisions the team members have advocated for and the composition of the unified decision-making teams, s/he should give an affirmation at the conclusion of the grid presentation. This sounds something like, "Thank you for advocating. I support you and your grid. These are now your decisions. Go make them."

When participants hear, "These are now your decisions. Go make them," their reaction is typically to look at their manager wide-eyed. Even though everyone has been working steadily toward this goal, most are actually surprised when they get to this point.

Whether it is spoken or not, people often go through the entire process waiting for the rug to be pulled out from under them. They listen and perform the activities without believing that power and decision-making will truly be redistributed, or that they will be given the opportunity to focus on the decisions that are most important to them and their organization, or that they will have official permission to execute on those decisions. When it happens, they often don't expect it. This is why the affirmation step is so important; it makes the process real, officially hands power to the participants, and gives them public permission to act.

Step 5:
Posting and Using the Grids

The last step in the process is to post the grids and use them. Posting is vital because it validates all the work that has gone into creating the Decision Clarity grids. Up until this point, participants may have focused only on their own grids without seeing the totality of the team's work. Posting the grids allows them to be seen officially, so they can be referred to and reinforced. If someone wants to be added to a particular grid, they can take the opportunity to advocate for their placement with the Decision-Maker.

Posting is done in many ways, but in our experience, we have seen value in affixing the grids to a wall. The actual physical presence of the grids sometimes trumps the ability to find them in your computer. If the grids are easily accessible by everyone, they're reminders of the process.

You can also use social media to create a page where the grids reside. You can likewise pass them out to everyone in your organization, or post them on a shared drive or in the cloud. Whichever way you choose to post the grids, they need to be in a place where people can see them. Making them available in multiple venues is also a good idea.

But how do you use them?

Aside from guiding the author in the pursuit of her or his new decision-making responsibilities, the grids can be used as an ongoing support tool in team meetings, one-on-ones, and performance reviews, or to assess progress and to reinforce the importance of certain decisions. The Decision Clarity grids function as a public declaration tool, and they can be used actively to keep the strategic motion of your organization (and the decisions that drive it) on track.

MANAGING TEAM INTERACTIONS

Now that the grids have been approved, it's important to speak to how Decision-Makers can best manage their decision-making teams. Having a plan to manage team interactions is critical, and our recommendation is to take each decision and meet with your Expert Advisor first. Ask this person for her or his overall thoughts on the decision you have to make.

Here are sample Expert Advisor questions to consider:

❖ Have you ever had to make a similar decision? What happened? What went into your decision? What was the outcome?

❖ What's your take on the factors I should weigh in making this decision?

❖ What is at stake for the organization in this decision?

❖ Is there anyone else besides the people on my grid I should talk to about this pending decision? (If the answer is yes, make note of their names and ask them if you can put them on your grid.)

Feel free to ask other questions as you see fit, then let your Expert Advisor know how s/he can help you going forward. Here are a few suggestions to increase your engagement with your Expert Advisor:

- ❖ "I'm weighing the following criteria_____ (insert criteria) to inform my decision-making. If there are other criteria that come to mind, please let me know."

- ❖ "What are the organizational pitfalls I should make note of and avoid when making my decision?"

- ❖ "What are the organizational benefits I should focus on as I consider the decision I have to make?"

- ❖ "I'd like to meet with you_____ (daily, every other day, weekly, every other week). Would you be willing to meet with me at that time?"

You may have noticed that you're not asking your Expert Advisor to make the decision you're both discussing. The decision is your responsibility and it's important to get started on the right foot. Your Expert Advisor is there to help you, and there are many ways you can engage this person. Choose an approach that works for you.

Next, meet with everyone in the Contributor group. Don't leave anyone out, and thank them for their willingness to contribute, refreshing their memory on the decision you're pursuing. Don't display any bias as to how you're going to decide or your reactions to their contribution. Your goal is to get their unvarnished input, so don't betray any early misgivings if they exist. Your job is to listen; whether or not you learn anything that will guide your decision-making remains to be seen. Here are sample Contributor questions to consider:

- ❖ Why did you advocate to be (or accept the assignment of being) a Contributor on this decision?

- ❖ What information or ideas would you like to contribute to my decision-making deliberations?

- ❖ Why is this contribution important to you?

- ❖ How would you like to be involved going forward?

Finally, meet with everyone in the Informed group. As with your Contributors, don't leave anyone out. When you meet with the members of this group, acknowledge their desire to be informed of your decision. Restate the decision you're pursuing, and listen to what they have to say, reassuring their need to be informed on a timely basis.

Here are sample Informed questions to consider:

❖ Why did you advocate to be (or accept the assignment of being) informed on this decision?

❖ How will this decision affect you if you're not informed?

❖ How would you like me to inform you of the decision I've made?

❖ How far in advance do you need to know my decision so you can best proceed?

If you need a Driver for your decision-making process, bring this person to your meetings. The more this person is familiar with the people in the Contributor and Informed categories, the more s/he can be of service to the decision.

Here are some final thoughts on managing the people on your unified decision-making team:

1. Don't make a decision before you've consulted with your team.

Of course, there are always emergencies, but making a decision on your grid without consulting with the people on the team will be experienced as a breach of trust.

2. Allow your team to have a voice and to fulfill their roles.

Honor the roles within the process. Listen to and make time for your Contributors; notify on a timely basis those who want to be Informed; take into consideration the ideas of your Expert Advisor. Building a team and then disregarding what they have to say will create bad blood in your decision-making ecosystem, so remember that your unified decision-making team wants to help you. Reap the benefits of their support. You don't have to take every piece of your team's advice; you simply have to acknowledge that you've heard it. If the people on your team think you're steering in the wrong direction, they can always bring up their frustration to the Expert Advisor.

3. Once down the path, don't stop.

As a result of championing this method, you've changed the power and decision-making model in your organization. Don't get cold feet. If you've made a commitment to this work, keep it. If a particular Decision-Maker isn't doing a good job, talk to that person; be clear about the quality of decision-making you expect from everyone, but don't implement this process and abandon it. Your people have made a historic leap to change their perspective. If you pull the rug out from under them, you will be left with a frustrated group of people whose trust has been damaged. They will then retreat and begrudgingly go back to the old ways of doing things.

FINAL THOUGHTS

The content in this chapter may seem overly prescriptive, but bear in mind that when you create a new decision-making culture and language in your organization, you have to be precise. The advantage of implementing this practice in the manner we've detailed here is that your team will be trained to work in a unified way. Everyone will be on the same page, and you won't be alone.

Yes, this process takes time and effort. And while it sometimes appears easier and quicker to make decisions in isolation and in a "one-off" fashion, the benefits of making unilateral decisions are an illusion. Having ambiguity about your decision-making process wastes far more time than the relatively few hours spent mastering this process. Deciding in advance who will make which decisions and then empowering each person (and their supporting cast) is an inherently better way to engage the talents of your team for the long-term benefit of the whole organization. As the wise African proverb states:

"If you want to go fast, go alone. If you want to go far, go together."

In the final chapter, we'll explore a key role in your new system that will ensure the method is working, that all remain on board, and that the process continues to run smoothly as your organization undergoes its transformation for the better.

KEY TAKEAWAYS

Publicly advocating for the decisions you want to make or support is an act of power and will create a transparent decision-making culture in your organization.

Each of us has implicit and largely unquestioned biases about who should be making which decisions in our organizations—we need to understand these and question their validity.

The "Free and Fair Participation Guarantee" will spark commitment and encourage the participation of all members of your team.

The process of reviewing Decision Clarity grids follows a format that ensures participation and dampens fear, consisting of:

- Opening Reassurance
- Setting the Rules
- Advocating and Getting Feedback
- Affirmation

As a Decision-Maker, once you've advocated for and received the necessary affirmation to proceed with making or supporting the decisions on your grid, it's important to manage the members of your decision-making team with gratitude and respect. This means:

- Don't make decisions until you've consulted with your team.
- Allow your team to fulfill their roles.
- Don't get cold feet and stop the process.

When your team is trained to work in a unified way, everyone will be on the same page, and you won't be alone—it's a win-win!

Self-advocacy creates true empowerment, allowing people to be better equipped to tackle the decisions for which they have advocated. Even if they aren't awarded a particular decision, they feel better for having the courage to speak up.

THE DECISION CLARITY ARCHITECT

At this juncture, you're likely wondering how this new system stays on track. How are deadlines met? How are the grids maintained? Who keeps everyone accountable? Not to worry—the answers to these questions and more are addressed within this chapter.

In Chapter 4, we outlined the four prominent leadership decision-making styles, those that typically surface when conflict or confusion boils up in organizations around decision-making—Autocrat, Appeaser, Avoider, and Micromanager. But there's a fifth style called the Decision Clarity Architect[14]. Unlike the other four, a healthy balance exists in this role, and this is the one that will serve you best in the nonprofit environment.

---

[14] The term "Decision Architect" has its origin in the book *Nudge: Improving Decisions About Health, Wealth and Happiness* by Richard Thaler and Cass Sunstein. They call the role "Choice Architect," but we have adapted it for the Decision Clarity practice.

WHAT DOES THE DECISION CLARITY ARCHITECT DO?

The role of Decision Clarity Architect (DCA) is a bold and brave position that provides oversight of the decision-making grids and encouragement of a positive decision-making climate. This is not a full-time job; the person in this role simply speaks to conflict and confusion that may arise, much like an air-traffic controller, ensuring that the organization's ecosystem (or the DCA's portion) runs smoothly. While this person assumes a greater leadership role in service to their nonprofit, it's important to note that s/he does not need to oversee communication or sharing of grids among departments, teams, or individuals, but merely establishes and maintains a fair playing field for everyone to flourish.

WHO IS BEST SUITED TO TAKE ON THIS ROLE?

The person who assumes this role should embody the following characteristics:

- ❖ A level of maturity and integrity

- ❖ Comfort being in a position of influence and willingness to focus his/her decision-making while enabling others to do the same

- ❖ Is unafraid to speak up and keep everyone on track in a positive way

- ❖ Is willing to point out conflict and confusion without being intimidated—or intimidating

- ❖ Always comes from a place of service

HOW MANY DECISION CLARITY ARCHITECTS DO WE NEED?

In what is considered a "smaller" nonprofit (50 people or less), one DCA will typically suffice. For those with more than 50 people, one architect per major group is recommended.

How Is the Decision Clarity Architect Appointed?

There are various ways to decide on who should be your Decision Clarity Architect(s), but the following steps will serve as an excellent guideline.

1. Does the executive director wish to assume this role?

In a smaller nonprofit, it may be a natural assumption for the executive director to take on this task, *if* s/he wishes; however, it is also an opportunity for the executive director to choose someone who has earned and would like an enhanced leadership role, possibly to groom him/her for a future executive director position.

2. If the executive director does not take on the role, how should the right person be determined?

The executive director should ask for volunteers, allowing people to self-advocate, and ensure that the candidates embrace all the characteristics listed on the previous page. The appointment of the best choice may then be determined by the executive director and presented at the team meeting.

Once your Decision Clarity Architect is determined, that person will need a framework in which to operate. We'll talk about that shortly; but first, let's take a look at a couple of vital points that this person will need to embrace.

> Keep in mind that the person MUST generally be respected by the members of the organization who will be taking guidance from him/her. The executive director shouldn't simply choose someone s/he favors and hope for the best; professionalism, kindness, and lack of arrogance coupled with a sincere desire to see everyone succeed in his/her positions is paramount in the Decision Clarity Architect.

The Imperative to "Think Different"

Boldness and bravery are not in short supply in nonprofits. Every day, people in this arena go to work and try to do the impossible. They fight against great odds to make a difference; they risk burnout for the opportunity to work for below-market pay to make progress on the largest problems confronting our society. They are the idealists who move our society forward. They battle against the odds to create a more just society, and they are often unrecognized and sometimes marginalized. With all the stress and challenges inherent in this work, many would think they are a little crazy to do what they do. But sometimes, you definitely need to be a little crazy to make a difference.

In early 1997, Steve Jobs returned to Apple after a twelve-year hiatus. While it may be hard to believe, Apple was a failing company at the time, short on cash and in desperate need of revitalizing its product and organization. Looking for a way to reposition Apple's brand, Jobs sought to relaunch the company. To begin the process, Jobs and his team worked with the creative team at TBWA/Chiat/Day and created the legendary "Think Different" campaign.

The print ads for this campaign featured black-and-white photos of people who have advanced civilization. Some of the individuals were Bob Dylan, Amelia Earhart, Thomas Edison, Mahatma Gandhi, and Jackie Robinson. Their pictures occupied full-page ads in newspapers and magazines, and on bus stops and billboards. Each picture had a small Apple logo and a two-word headline: "Think Different." The wording drove grammarians crazy, but it was the campaign that got Apple back on track.

In conjunction with the "Think Different" print campaign, Apple ran a television ad entitled, "Here's to the Crazy Ones," narrated by Richard Dreyfuss. It won numerous awards and lionized the people in the print campaign as beacons who advanced the human cause. It likewise emphasized utilizing the energy you already bring to work every day. Here is a short excerpt:

> Here's to the crazy ones.
> The misfits. The rebels. The troublemakers.
> They're not fond of rules. And they have no respect for the status quo.
> While some may see them as the crazy ones, we see genius.
> Because the people who are crazy enough to think they can change the world …
> are the ones who do.

Read that last line again. Do you recognize yourself in that description? We bet you do. Whether you're bringing clean drinking water to countries in Africa, or battling against AIDS, or shining a light on the pernicious nature of child abuse, or trying to improve student achievement in the inner city or rural communities, you've taken on a role and a challenge that few people would want. Sometimes you have to be a "rebel" and a "troublemaker"; sometimes you must rail against "the status quo," because otherwise nothing will change.

THE RIGHT ECOSYSTEM

There are not many people who are willing to face the odds you face every day and keep at it. You want to change the world and you're crazy enough to try, and Decision Clarity is one of the tools that can help you do it. But it will only grow and flourish in the right ecosystem.

If you want Decision Clarity to be sustained in your organization, you have to make it happen. Cultivating the right ecosystem takes conscious strategy and effort because human beings are funny. They need reinforcement, encouragement, and consistency, even when the changes they are implementing are what they want to see happen. For this reason, we offer you some strategies and guidelines to help you reinforce the new behaviors and attitudes blossoming in your organization.

REINFORCEMENT STRATEGIES FOR DCAS

There are four main strategies that will help you implement, reinforce, and sustain the use of Decision Clarity with your staff.

Strategy 1: Be Consistent
Model decision clarity and others will too.

As a leader, all eyes are on you. When you're a Decision Clarity Architect, you can't talk about the importance of clarifying decision-making and then not act in accordance with the principles of the practice. You can't urge people to focus their decision-making, and then allow yourself to remain unfocused. You can't give decision-making authority to someone and then take it away at the first whiff of trouble.

In the nonprofit world, it can be tempting to rush to the next fire and create an exception "just this one time." Don't do it. No matter how much pressure you feel, stick with the process. Leaders sometimes think they can operate "under the radar." Don't fool yourself. Your team is watching your every step. There are few actions you can take that won't be noticed.

Your team will pay particular attention if they feel you're holding them to a standard you aren't willing to meet. If the other people in your ecosystem see that you talk a good game but are unwilling to play by the rules you've established, the renewed decision-making ecosystem you've created will crumble. So be consistent. By doing so, you will create the safety that people need to be effective in their self-advocacy, and in their jobs.

The bottom line is: if, as a leader, you advocate and encourage others to do so, everyone else will follow. If you say no to the less-important decisions you encounter every day and focus on the bigger ones, others will find the bravery to do so as well. But most importantly, you want to use the Decision Clarity practice to openly and clearly advocate for the decisions you want to make or support, as well as the decisions you want to give away. If you do this, others will follow your lead.

As a leader, it's crucial for you to set expectations as to how decisions will get made. You need to be clear with everyone in your ecosystem about the level of thoughtfulness, cooperation, diligence, and speed you want to see from the individuals who are making decisions.

You also need to set expectations for how people in support roles will operate. If someone has signed up as a Contributor and hasn't participated, you need to speak up. If an Expert Advisor isn't available to her or his Decision-Maker, you need to step in. Be mindful of the change you want to make in your organization, and make sure that people are fulfilling the roles they've signed up for. This monitoring doesn't take a lot of time, but it's invaluable as a reinforcement strategy. Stick with the program. Be consistent. Be a model.

Know that your job is indeed to make the decisions on your grid, but it's also to create the best decision-making ecosystem so that others can do the same. Like an architect, you need to be someone who is responsible for creating the right overall structure, not merely someone who is interested only in their own room in the house.

Strategy 2: Maintain Demeanor
Create decision-making confidence.

One advantage of using Decision Clarity is that for the first time you know all the decisions that have to be made and who will make them. This alone should engender a feeling of calm. But in order to fully implement Decision Clarity, you must initially quiet the anxiety in your head about the decisions others are going to make. Decision Clarity requires a new mindset; you now have to trust people to make (or support) the decisions they've advocated for. It's one of the great ironies of nonprofit service that we trust our processes and our clients, but we sometimes have trouble fully trusting our colleagues.

Fear of failure often erodes trust and self-advocacy, and Decision Clarity will be difficult to sustain if trust is in short supply. You build trust by giving people the chance to actually do their jobs, and make (or support) the decisions they've signed up for. Assure them that you will let them do their work.

One of the great truisms in life is that people will often mirror what they see. This is particularly the case when we refer to organizational leadership. Given our human propensity to look for behavioral cues, if you're calm in the face of decision-making, your team will quickly understand that this is the way they should be as well.

Especially in the beginning, give people the space to experiment with the decisions they've advocated to make. If people believe their judgments and decisions are being overly scrutinized, they will likely shrink from asserting themselves, or bristle in anger that "they always knew this wouldn't work." This is not a good outcome. So maintain a calm and inquiring mind, and give the people who have advocated for specific roles the space to fulfill them.

If a particular decision is not forthcoming, or if it's lacking in your estimation, by all means address your concerns directly, but do so in a calm manner, and after the person has had a chance to explain what is happening. If someone is suffering from indecision, encourage him or her to take a deep breath, review the choices at hand, consult with the people on his or her team, and make a decision. Your job is to coach and support people to make the right decisions, not to take over.

As a leader, you have to be able to live with the decisions you give to others. It's tough to watch someone falter, and tougher when you know that the organization and your clients are counting on a good outcome. Keep in mind, however, that how you handle the failure of others will be watched by everyone in your ecosystem. If you wail and lose control, you will set the effort back. Nurture the people who take their decision-making roles seriously; give them another chance if need be. People do learn, and if you can manage to cope with an occasional mistake, everyone will grow from it. Take a deep breath ... and then take another.

If someone is truly incapable of making (or supporting) the decisions for which they've advocated, be forthright about that challenge. Ask the Decision-Maker whether s/he wants to go forward. If not, gather the team and ask for a volunteer to serve in this capacity. Be straightforward and unafraid about these challenges. Your calm demeanor will create trust and confidence.

Strategy 3: Speak the Truth

Point out decision-making bottlenecks.

Being a Decision Clarity Architect requires that you assume the responsibility of selflessly identifying the decision-making bottlenecks that prevent your team, group, or organization from making decisions. Your job is to respectfully yet directly point these bottlenecks out and push to eliminate them.

Everyone in your organization knows where the decision-making bottlenecks are located. People may roll their eyes when a person with challenges in this arena is installed as a Decision-Maker, or look aghast when long-simmering discordance between groups is allowed to fester without resolution. Sometimes, bottlenecks occur because the decision being considered is simply too complex for rapid resolution.

But more often than not, bottlenecks crop up because the person entrusted with the decision can't focus on it, and a lack of trust or ego prevents them from acknowledging their overloaded situation.

To resolve roadblocks, the Decision Clarity Architect must adopt a brave demeanor and an unbiased perspective. Having assumed this role with the permission of your organization, you have nothing to lose by giving voice to the roadblock before you; if you're the executive director, you can muster your courage and point out what everyone knows: your organization is stymied and it would be best to acknowledge and address this challenge.

So what language can you use to address these roadblocks? Being direct is always best, as in the following example:

"I've noticed that the decision to _____ has not been made."

Then ask:

"What's slowing our decision-making on this issue?"

"When do you think this decision can be made?"

"What will it take to get this decision made?"

When you take the time to point out the roadblock, often this is enough to spur action. If your team has committed to implementing Decision Clarity, you have the permission you need to bring up these issues. Be in service to the larger goal, and don't be content with confusion or conflict.

Strategy 4: Encourage Accountability
Model good communication and you'll receive it in return.

While your strategic plan may be collecting dust on your bookshelf, your completed Decision Clarity grids allow you and the other members of your team to keep track of the decisions that have to be made in your ecosystem. Refer to them often; bring copies to meetings. Create a master grid that incorporates everyone's grid into one and keep it updated regularly using a spreadsheet program or online tool, such as Google Docs. This will enable you to increase the level of accountability for yourself and for everyone else on your team.

The Decision Clarity grids are an excellent way to track and project-manage the decisions that are important to your organization. In your one-on-one meetings with team members, you now have a structure and a language you can use for getting to the point quickly. You can say, "Will you be able to make the _____ decision by_____?" without having to wonder whether you and the person in front of you are aligned. You can say, "What are the challenges you're encountering in making the _____ decision?" Or, "Are you being given the chance to contribute to the _____ decision? Do you feel that your input is being listened to?" This method creates a consistent language you can use to streamline decision-making on a day-by-day basis.

In your team meetings, you can go around the room to ask for updates on every decision on your team's grids (or on the master). This is an excellent way to verify that those who have advocated for roles are moving forward, but it's also a way to make sure that your staff are cooperating with and accountable to each other.

You can also use Decision Clarity to increase accountability and communication throughout your organization. In your "town hall" meetings with the entire staff, you can post a grid that represents your nonprofit's top ten decisions and give updates on progress.

As we've highlighted before, accountability can take a back seat when a nonprofit wants to maintain a family feeling; pointing out accountability failures can be seen as too threatening. Using the Decision Clarity grids in a public forum enables you and everyone else in your ecosystem to be clear about what everyone is doing. It's all out in the open, and communication becomes a priority rather than an afterthought.

Managing Your Grids' Evolution

Clearly, as decisions are made, they are moved off the grid(s) to make room for new decisions, giving the entire team a strong sense of accomplishment. While individual managers and staff should review their grids as they see fit, the DCA should serve as a catalyst for determining when it is most beneficial for the organization to have a comprehensive review. Some organizations like to meet once a month; others find every quarter suitable. You may determine that holding a special meeting once a month to evaluate where the organization is in terms of high-impact decisions is helpful as well. You don't however, want the DCA responsibilities to overtake that person's main position, so it's important that s/he strike a balance and keep the architect role manageable. In short, whatever works for your nonprofit—which you may not know until you experiment a bit—is the course you should follow for maximum results.

It will also be necessary to reevaluate your decision lists periodically. As your nonprofit evolves and turnover occurs, the DCA will need to facilitate new inventorying and prioritizing activities to stay up to date. If you have a training director, this person may take on the responsibility of explaining the Decision Clarity system to new hires. For example, once a role in the organization has a solid list of typical decisions, the new person can assume those decisions. If that person doesn't seem suited for all of them, decisions may need to be redirected for a time. Again, this structure and practice will depend on your particular organization and its needs.

FREQUENTLY ASKED QUESTIONS ABOUT THE DECISION CLARITY ARCHITECT ROLE

Does the person who assumes or is appointed the DCA role receive a raise in pay?

If the DCA is the executive director, the answer is likely no; it would naturally fall on that person to improve the organization's overall performance, so this would simply be part of facilitating that goal. If someone's been given this added responsibility, it will be up to the executive director and the board to decide if a pay raise is feasible. Whether or not you're able to give a raise, however, it's important to emphasize the enhanced leadership opportunity and possibility for promotion that the position affords. Having greater influence and helping to move your nonprofit forward has its own reward, and while more money is always nice, your staff should understand that may not be reasonable.

Should the DCA serve a "minimum term"?

It's always possible that the person may decide the role carries more responsibility than s/he wanted, but it's also prudent to expect that person to remain in the role long enough to give it a real chance. It may simply take a little time to get in the groove of being the DCA, and that person should have the executive director's and staff's full support to adjust to the responsibility. As such, we recommend the person give the role at least three months; if at the end of the term the person wishes to step down, it would be incumbent upon the executive director or other leadership to initiate nominations or appointments for a new person to assume the role.

What if the executive director assumes the DCA role and then decides s/he would prefer to hand it over to someone else?

As in the prior scenario, it should be no problem to put the role up for nomination and allow others to self-advocate for the role.

How often should you select a new Decision Clarity Architect?

As with any position one holds for a long time, enthusiasm can sometimes wane and a new challenge is necessary to maintain engagement; no one wants to be stuck in one role indefinitely, and it's no different for the DCA. While the position does regularly present new opportunities for learning and for varying participation with the staff, it's also a good idea to consider rotating the role among those who show the maturity, integrity, experience, and interest in assuming it. In any case, continuity is as important as innovation, so you'll want to keep that in mind as you decide how often to change out the role, voluntarily or not.

In sum, taking on the role of Decision Clarity Architect allows for a great deal of positive influence to be spread throughout your organization, as well as creating an exciting opportunity to grow as a leader. What's more, the person will be a key player in strengthening your nonprofit by attracting and retaining talented staff, saving both time and money, and cultivating a diverse team of leaders from the bottom up. With tangible goals, clarity on who's making which decisions, and the new sense of value and empowerment your team will feel, the DCA is rewarded with pride and accomplishment for guiding a practice that delivers a true win-win—not only for the members of the organization, but for the cherished beneficiaries you work so hard to serve.

KEY TAKEAWAYS

The DCA must consistently model Decision Clarity—and encourage others to do so—to create confidence and elicit the best response in your organization.

The Decision Clarity Architect oversees the decision-making grids, deadlines, team relations, and expected results while speaking to the potential conflict and roadblocks that may keep your organization from fulfilling its potential.

The person who assumes the DCA role should:

- have an appropriate level of maturity and integrity
- be comfortable in a position of influence
- be willing to focus on his/her decision-making while enabling others to do the same
- be unafraid to speak up and keep everyone on track in a positive way
- not view leadership as "ordering people around"
- always come from a place of service

One DCA is sufficient for organizations with 50 members or fewer; larger nonprofits may require one for each major group.

If the executive director doesn't assume the role, the DCA can be appointed by the executive director or nominated by him/her or staff and voted on.

The ability to "think different" is paramount in an evolving organization, and the DCA is a leader in that thought process.

The four DCA strategies are:

- Be consistent.
- Maintain demeanor.
- Speak the truth.
- Encourage accountability.

As decisions are made, the DCA will need to periodically reevaluate the grids, deleting the completed decisions and adding new ones.

CONCLUSION

We know that as a nonprofit leader, board member, or staff person, you have enormous heart and commitment to your mission. To use words from the Apple campaign, you are the "misfits," the "rebels," and the "troublemakers" who make a difference to our society. Your team is made up of people dedicated to a cause, and they need to be engaged and consistently reinvigorated in their work; each of you needs to feel you have a great stake in the organizations you serve—and what underlies all of it is the ability to "think different" about power and decision-making.

We understand that any change management process takes faith—and faith can be described as being able to take a first step, even when you don't see the whole path. You want it to work, you *think* it will work, but in the end, you have to take that first step without knowing *for sure* how it will all pan out. The purpose of this book has been to guide you through a method that will help you take the first step, and the next step, and the next.

With the blueprint you hold in your hands, you now have the insight, activities, steps, and guided conversations to move your organization and everyone in it to a more harmonious place, one that will reduce fear, enhance confidence, mitigate conflict, and ultimately instill more joy, pride, accountability, and value in every member of your organization.

If you have the courage to foster the ability to "think different" as a role model and a leader—in whatever capacity you currently hold in your nonprofit—imagine how much more good you can do—better.

INDEX

advocate(d)/advocating, i, 2, 5, 11, 17, 21, 32, 34, 36, 85, 98, 114–117, 120, 124–125, 135, 143, 162, 164, 170, 174–184, 187, 189, 190, 192, 195–196, 202–203, 205–206, 209–210, 212, 213–214, 216–218, 220–224, 226–227, 230, 236–238, 240

Amodeo, John, 16

Appeaser, 89, 105, 231

Apple, (Inc.), 234, 245

Autocrat, 88–91, 105, 231

Avoider, 90, 105, 231

Barnett, Thomas, 93

beliefs, 24–25, 32, 54–45, 47, 53–54, 56, 95

bias(es), ii, 4–5, 30, 32–33, 47, 91, 124, 131, 158, 215–216, 226, 230, 239

CEID (Center for Early Intervention on Deafness), 52

Charles, Vignetta, 48

Chronicle of Philanthropy, 48

Commongood Careers, Inc., 110, 142

communicating for clarity, 116

conflict, 1–2, 13, 15–16, 22, 24, 33–38, 53, 71, 85–91, 93–102, 104, 105, 113, 115, 127, 154, 174, 210, 220–221, 231–232, 239, 244, 246

Contributor, 118, 120, 176, 178, 192–195, 202–204, 206–209, 214, 226–227, 236

Cuddy, Amy, 187–188

D-E-C-I-D model, 117, 120, 210

Decision Clarity, i–ii, 4–5, 37, 42, 45, 52, 82–83, 87, 94, 104, 105, 109–110, 112–114, 116–119, 120, 121–122, 125, 127–129, 131–132, 134–135, 137, 149, 156, 162, 169–170, 174, 177, 180–181, 189, 190, 192, 208–210, 212, 235, 236–237, 239–241, 244

grids, 112–113, 116, 120, 142, 169, 182, 191–194, 196, 198, 201, 204, 209–211, 212, 213, 216, 220, 224–225, 230, 239–240

Decision Clarity Architect (DCA), 231–233, 235, 238–239, 241–243, 244

decision fatigue, 160–161

decision-maker(s), 24, 32, 48, 117–118, 120, 143, 151, 154, 158, 165, 169, 177–178, 180, 183, 192–196, 202, 204–209, 214, 224–225, 228, 230, 236, 238

decision-making, i–ii, 1–5, 9–21, 22, 23–36, 38–45, 48, 50, 54, 56–57, 58, 59, 62, 64, 68–81, 83, 84, 86–91, 93, 95–99, 101, 104, 105, 109–110, 112–114, 116, 120, 124–127, 130–131, 133–136, 137, 141–144, 146, 148–150, 151, 155–156, 159, 160–163, 165–166, 170, 171, 175–181, 187, 189, 190, 192, 196, 203, 206–211, 213–216, 218, 220, 223, 225–228, 230, 231–232, 235–240, 244, 245

decisions
  high-impact, 115, 139, 154–156, 158–163, 167, 171, 182, 194, 196–198, 200–201, 210, 212, 213, 241
  inventory(ing), 113–115, 120, 139–145, 148, 150, 151, 167, 170, 192, 197–198
  maintenance, 154–159, 163, 171
  prioritize/prioritizing, 18, 113–115, 120, 145, 150, 153–156, 159, 160–162, 165, 167, 169–170, 171, 174, 182–183, 185, 192, 200, 201–203

diversity, 3, 16, 94–96, 101, 105

Driver, 118, 120, 176, 178, 192–196, 202, 204, 208–209, 214, 227

dysfunctional decision-making models, 31

dysfunctional leadership styles (*see* Appeaser, Autocrat, Avoider, Micromanager)

ecosystem, ii, 57, 59, 61, 62–64, 68, 70–83, 84, 86, 88, 90, 94, 97–98, 100, 104, 113, 123, 125, 150, 156, 170, 206, 227, 232, 235–238, 240

Ellis, Jill, 52

executive director(s), i, ii, 1-2, 10–12, 14–15, 20–21, 22, 23–25, 31–34, 38–42, 52, 60, 63, 65, 70–73, 76, 87–88, 90–94, 96–98, 101–103, 105, 116, 118–119, 121–122, 124–125, 131–135, 137, 143, 153, 170, 174–176, 180–181, 195, 203, 207, 211, 233, 239, 241–242, 244

Expert Advisor, 118, 120, 176–177, 192–195, 202–204, 206–209, 214, 225–228, 236

fear of conflict, 13, 15, 22, 174

fear of failure, 12–13, 15, 22, 32, 44, 53, 98, 174, 237

fear of rejection, 2, 13, 16–17, 22. 173–174

Ferguson Problem, 3

Gallup, (Inc.), 216

Gandhi, Mahatma, 135, 234

GreatSchools, 139, 159

Harvard Business Review, 170, 215
Harvard Management Update, 187

Iceberg, 24–25, 58
Informed, 118, 120, 176, 178, 192–196, 202–204, 207–209, 214, 227
IPAC (model), i, 114, 120

Jensen, Michael, 187
Jobs, Steve, 170, 234

leadership team, 10, 28, 31, 52, 60, 65, 70, 75–77, 84, 91–92, 97–98, 105, 121, 124

micromanager, 91, 105, 231
Miller, B.J., 10

Nelson, Matthew, 139
New York Times, The , 160
nonprofit
 board/board member(s), ii, 1–2, 5, 10–11, 18, 21, 23–24, 28, 31, 39–41, 46, 49, 52, 56, 60, 65, 70–75, 84,
  88, 90–92, 94–97, 100–103, 105, 109, 119, 120, 121, 132–135, 137, 143, 146, 153, 158, 170, 176, 181, 203,
  211, 241, 245
 clients, 14–15, 60, 67, 70, 79–80, 84, 99, 122, 153, 217, 237–238
 funders, 14, 52, 67, 70, 80, 84, 99, 146

Pentagon's New Map, The, 95
power, i–ii, 1–5, 9–11, 13–21, 22, 23–36, 38–39, 41–42, 44, 48, 50–57, 58, 59–62, 68, 70–71, 78–79, 83, 84,
 86–91, 93–101, 104, 109, 113–114, 124–126, 131, 133, 135–136, 137, 139, 143, 155, 173–177, 179–181, 187–189,
 190, 191–192, 205, 209–211, 212, 216, 218, 223–224, 228, 230, 245
Preston, Caroline, 48
privilege, i–ii, 47, 94–96, 101–103, 105

race, i–ii, 13, 16, 32, 94–95, 102–103, 189
Ruesga, Albert, 48

Schramm, J.B., 15, 55
self-advocate/self-advocacy, 113, 170, 173–180, 182, 186–187, 189, 190, 233, 236–237, 242
Sills, Judith, 56

strategic plan(s), 1, 10, 140, 146, 196–197, 212, 239
Styers, David, 96
Subway, 173–174, 179, 221

Tierney, John, 160

unified decision-making team(s), 21, 120, 196, 206, 210, 213, 220, 223, 227

volunteer(s), 1, 60, 66, 70, 78–79, 84, 94, 100–103, 105, 140–141, 146, 233, 238

Zen Hospice Project, 10, 140

ACKNOWLEDGMENTS

Deciding to write a book is an important first step in the creative process, but figuring out how to do it is yet another challenge. Despite my passion for the subject, this book would not exist without the support readily offered by so many people. A "thank you" does not begin to describe the debt I feel to all who are listed below. Each one of them decided to become "contributors" to this effort and I'm so grateful for all they have done.

Joel Orr was my book coach, with whom I spent the better part of 2013 discussing the ideas in the book and wrestling with early outlines. He very patiently reviewed my early musings and got me ready to write.

Taylor Ray, who served as my developmental editor, worked hand in glove with me to create the manuscript, and the book was definitely shaped by her insights and commitment. Stacey Aaronson then polished the manuscript and designed the cover and interior—the book's accessibility is directly related to Stacey's efforts. Both Taylor and Stacey were fantastic collaborators who added greatly to the book.

G.E. Gallas added insight, humor, and clarity to the content as my wonderful illustrator. My thanks also to illustrator Paul Wood and the *Harvard Business Review* for allowing me to use Paul's "dog/cat" illustration in Chapter 11.

A special thank you and acknowledgment to my partner and friend, Diedra Barber. Diedra is an incredible collaborator and I'm very lucky for all the support and insight she so readily offers.

Sharon Bially and DeAnna Jacobsen at BookSavvy PR have been great to work with, and I appreciate all their efforts to promote the book.

My thanks also to Jessica Robinson Gemm, Melissa Jones, and Felicia Martin, who collaborated with me on our early Decision Clarity engagements.

A number of nonprofit people read the manuscript and provided valuable feedback. Included in this category are Paul Collins, Jill Ellis, Judy Madden, Sheldon Maye, B.J. Miller, Jamila Brown-Mindingall, Robyn Scates, and Kathleen Yazbak.

A special thank you to my friends and colleagues at College Summit for graciously providing me with the intellectual property rights for the early Decision Clarity material I developed while on staff.

My thanks to Cassie Scarano of Commongood Careers (CGC) and James Weinberg and Dana Hagenbuch, then of CGC, for their support of the initial survey we launched on the CGC web site.

Other collaborators/supporters include:

Sam Barry, Jo Beaton, Idalin "Abby" Bobe, David Brodwin, Lauren Carpenter, Chip Conley, Hugh Dubberly, Barbara Friedman, Carmine Gallo, Ginger Holt, Guy Kawasaki, Amanda Kimball, Karla Monterroso, Nancy Morano, Paul Pruneau, Doug Solomon, and the staff at the Starbucks at 4th and King Street in San Francisco.

Dani Shapiro's book, *Still Writing: The Perils and Pleasures of a Creative Life*, provided solace as I immersed myself in writing and rewriting. Steven Pressfield's books, *The War of Art* and *The Warrior's Ethos* provided inspiration and helped me persevere. These authors are magical and I urge all to read them.

Izetta Autumn Mobley was on my team at College Summit, and I learned a great deal from her about race and class that served me well as I created this book. Thank you.

My thanks to all the nonprofit leaders who made the time to be interviewed for this book and for the insights they provided: Julie Castro Abrams, Cynthia Chavez, Jack Cohen, Justina Cross, Alison DeJung, Amanda Feinstein, Elana Gary, Larry Griffin, Mark Hecker, Darian Rodriguez Heyman, Linda Hill, Alan Kirschner, Suzanne McKechnie Klahr, Jan Masaoka, Mona Masri, Cynthia Murray, Michele Ozumba, Marina Park, Judy Patrick, Stephen Pratt, Monica Pressley, Catherine Pyke, Marc Rand, Mary Rogier, J.B. Schramm, Premal Shah, Beth Sirull, Eric Sloan, David Smith, Marc Spencer, Vidya Sundaram, David Styers, Peter Tavernise, Kat Taylor, Dena Trujillo, Bob Uyeki, Jill Vialet, Judy Weisinger, and Tom Wilson.

Thanks also go to the leadership teams, staff, and board members of our clients who have made the brave decision to examine their power and decision-making practices so they can do more good. Better. Thank you for your trust.

Finally, my thanks to Heather for all her support during this period. Her unwavering encouragement made all the difference. She makes everything better.

ABOUT THE AUTHOR

STEVE SCHEIER is CEO and founder of Scheier+Group, a consulting firm dedicated to helping organizations clarify power and streamline decision-making so they can do more good. During his 20-plus years of experience as a human resources and nonprofit leader, Steve has observed the stifling power dynamics that impact organizations; as such, he is a firm believer in driving decision-making down so that institutions can gain the maximum benefit from their human resources and increase the focus of their leaders.

Prior to founding Scheier+Group in 2010, Steve served as vice president of human assets and training at the education nonprofit College Summit, and president at the Entrepreneurs' Foundation. His private-sector experience includes serving as a vice president of human resources at Food.com and CKS Group. In addition, he worked at Apple for nine years, during which he served as product introduction manager for the 1984 launch of the Macintosh, was responsible for the company's first statewide computer donation program to schools, and led Apple's Creative Services organization. In his last position at Apple, Steve served as the director of marketing for the K–12 education sector. Prior to working at Apple, Steve worked for both the federal and state governments, serving in the National Institute of Education and The California Department of Education, and he was chief of staff to the chair of the California State Assembly's Ways and Means Committee.

Steve holds a B.A. in History and an M.A. in Education Policy from the University of California, Berkeley. When not working on power and decision-making issues with nonprofits and entrepreneurial startups, Steve enjoys his life in San Francisco. He invites you to follow his blog at scheiergroup.com.

ABOUT SCHEIER+GROUP

Headed by Steve Scheier and Diedra Barber, Scheier+Group believes in making the world a better place, and they have a big space in their hearts for mission-driven organizations. Nonprofits and social-impact companies attract the smartest, most committed people at all levels, but they often need help making the most of the people they have so they can better deliver on their mission. We not only work with these organizations through our Jumpstart and Boot Camp programs, but we also speak at conferences and to individual organizations to share our message of clarified power and decision-making.

Do More Good. Better. was created as a blueprint to shepherd nonprofit leaders through a process of positive transformation. However, if you prefer to have more personalized guidance and wish to work with us directly, you'll have access to our 1x1 coaching and technology, boosting the implementation of Decision Clarity in your nonprofit. Organizations that work with us:

- ❖ attract a diverse and talented staff, which strengthens every aspect of their nonprofit

- ❖ save both time and money in training and execution of tasks, big and small, because their decision-making structure is clear to everyone

- ❖ enjoy higher employee retention and commitment to the cause

- ❖ cultivate a more diverse team of leaders from the bottom up, which benefits both the organization and the sector they serve

- ❖ discover faster and more effective decision-making and better collaboration among all team members

If we can be of service to you, please fill out the contact form on the Scheier+Group site at www.scheiergroup.com/contact, and we'll be in touch to see how we can best help.

CPSIA information can be obtained
at www.ICGtesting.com
Printed in the USA
FSOW03n0807010218
44067FS